RAISED EMBROIDERY

A PRACTICAL GUIDE TO DECORATIVE STUMPWORK

RAISED EMBROIDERY

A PRACTICAL GUIDE TO DECORATIVE STUMPWORK

BARBARA AND ROY HIRST

MEREHURST

We dedicate this book to our young seventeenth-century forbears who made it possible.

Published in 1993 by Merehurst Limited, Ferry House,
51-57 Lacy Road, Putney, London, SW15 1PR

Reprinted 1993 , 1994 (twice) , 1996

Edited by Diana Brinton
Designed by Bill Mason
Photography by Stewart Grant

Typeset by Rowland Phototypesetting Limited,
Bury St Edmunds, Suffolk
Colour separation by Scantrans, Singapore
Printed in Singapore by C. S. Graphics

CONTENTS

INTRODUCTION

The highly individual type of embroidery demonstrated in this book flourished in its original form for only a few decades of the 17th century. Although it is often known to collectors and modern embroiderers as stumpwork, there is every reason to believe that, in common with the professional embroiderer of the 15th and 16th centuries, the 17th-century domestic embroiderer referred to her work, quite simply, as 'raised', 'embossed', or perhaps 'embosted' embroidery.

Its capacity for conveying life and humour, and the way in which it combines many different embroidery and lacemaking techniques make this type of work an ideal vehicle for modern embroiderers seeking to achieve similar effects in a contemporary idiom. Fascinating and enjoyable in themselves, 17th-century raised embroideries provide a rich source of ideas and techniques, as we hope this book will show.

RAISED EMBROIDERY

The particular type of embroidery that is the subject of this book flourished between about 1640 and 1680, during the reigns of Charles I and Charles II, though work of an earlier date does exist, and embroidery in this style continued until the end of the 17th century and a little later. It is generally regarded as a domestic embroidery, but there is little precise information about the many people who stitched the great quantity of panels, boxes and caskets, mirror surrounds, cushions, book covers and other items. Many were the work of young girls, such as Hannah Smith, who completed her casket at the age of 14, or the even more precocious Martha Edlin, who was but 11 years old.

The enigmatic term 'stumpwork' is disliked by some people, though it has its uses in defining work of this very precise and limited period. The term is probably an invention of the late 19th century, its first known use being in 1894. Lady Marian Alford had earlier referred to the style as 'work on the stamp', while Rees *Cyclopedia* defines embroideries 'on the stamp or stump' as those in which the figures are high and prominent, and supported by cotton, hair or wool.

The reason why this new name for raised embroidery should have been coined in the 19th century remains to be discovered, and it certainly provides a puzzle for the enquiring mind. References to wooden moulds (stumps), used for relief padding, or the printing (stamping) of designs on the ground fabric were used, not very plausibly, to justify the term early in this century. More recently, it has been suggested that the French word 'estompe', meaning embossed, might be worthy of exploration.

The Pear Tree Stitch Sampler *was worked in the traditional style by the authors.*

The embroiderer's initials can sometimes be found on raised embroidery, and even — more rarely — some proof of her name. An embroidered bookmark, pen or knife holder, and a purse, were found inside the casket. The purse bears the embroidered inscription 'Jean Morris is name 1660', and it seems likely that she made all four items. The raised embroidery on the sides and lid of the casket depict Old Testament scenes from the life of Joseph. Courtesy of Christies, South Kensington. Size: 14cm x 35cm x 25cm (5½in x 14in x 10in)

WHAT IS RAISED EMBROIDERY?

Although domestic stumpwork/raised embroidery embraces flatwork and a large variety of stitches, the definitive features of this style might be summed up as follows:

- The use of 'needlemade fabrics' in the form of needlelace (buttonhole stitch), and pieces of embroidery which are known as slips, and are made separately. Both overlap embossed areas and, in the case of the former, fly freely above the face of the ground fabric and the embossed images.
- The use of wires and vellum, bound with silk and other threads, to provide texture and decorative relief features.
- The application of a wealth of supplementary ornamentation in a variety of available materials, including embroidered silk fabrics, pearls, beads, semi-precious stones, real hair, feathers, mica, metal threads/strips, braids, silk-bound and painted purl, and in one rare example, in the Victoria and Albert Museum, London, a fragment of woven tapestry.
- A mass of minute details, all set within a miniature scale.
- The strong use of figurative subjects within an otherwise natural design.

The principal features, lifted above the flatwork, will have the character of embossed work, but small, selected items will burst out with even greater exuberance, and will be worked completely in the round.

Almost without exception, extant work reveals remarkable inventiveness and dexterity, displayed in a myriad of small embroidered slips and constructed artifacts, and an even greater ingenuity in their assembly into a finished piece of work.

The design of this box lid illustrates the story of David and Bathsheba, wife of Uriah the Hittite, which can be read in 2 Samuel XI. It is copied from an engraving in Thesaurus Sacrarum Historiarum Veteris Testimenti, *published in Antwerp in 1585, by Gerard de Jode. Some 42 other embroideries have been identified by Nancy Graves Cabot as having been inspired by this source. From the Embroiderers' Guild Collection – photographed by Julia Hedgecoe. Size: 28cm x 39cm x 14cm (11in x 15½in x 5½in)*

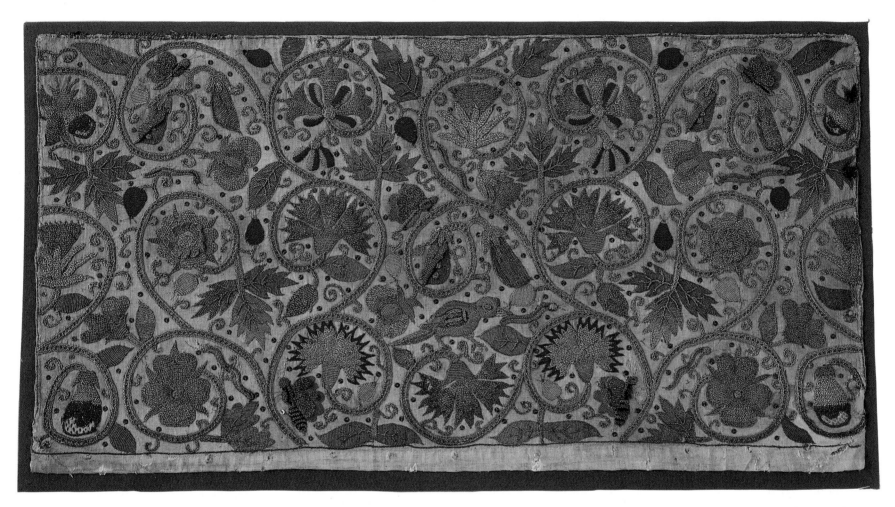

HOW DID THIS EMBROIDERY ORIGINATE AND DEVELOP?

The fully developed nature of almost all historic stumpwork embroidery gives the impression that this domestic style of work arrived on the embroidery scene in 17th-century England suddenly, some time around 1640, with few obvious signs of earlier stages of evolution. Some writers link the birth of this style with the nuns of Little Gidding, near Cambridge, in England, but John L. Nevinson, researching in the 1930s, failed to find proof of any such connections. It seems much more likely that young 17th-century embroiderers were predominantly influenced by two distinct but already well-developed styles of embroidery.

This small, early 17th-century panel is rich in needlelace stitches. The peas are in relief, and flower petals and butterfly wings are 'in the air'. This style of work is a prelude to stumpwork. From the Embroiderers' Guild Collection – photographed by Julia Hedgecoe.

For about two centuries before the emergence of domestic stumpwork in England, professional figurative work was being produced in Europe. Many examples of this earlier embroidery, which featured fine softly-sculptured detailing, with applied and padded fabrics and with additional laid threads, can be seen in today's collections. Much of the work is confined to ecclesiastical vestments, to pictures and – in

Germany – to shields produced for crafts guilds. A cushion in this style was produced for Winchester College Chapel as late as 1636 by one Mr Cheaves.

A second and perhaps more important influence came from needlelace, which flourished and developed during the Elizabethan period. In essence produced by detached buttonhole stitch, with variations that often lifted it above the ground fabric, it was well established by the end of the 16th century.

While domestic stumpwork embroiderers never achieved the fine sculptural form of their forebears, nor stitched quite so exquisitely as the Elizabethans, they made their own inimitable contribution to embroidery when they created a marriage between these two earlier divergent styles of work.

THE PICTURES AND DESIGNS OF STUMPWORK

A researcher can be confused, as well as charmed, by the profusion of pictorial and decorative detail on stumpwork embroideries, and also by the strange absence of scale. Flowers, insects, animals and trees jostle for position in scrapbook fashion and mix indiscriminately with fountains and fish, country mansions and castles, and costumed figures, as well as lions and leopards, all in an improbable English countryside, where the sun and moon shine at one and the same time.

Some Victorian writers attributed these strange designs to the young girls who stitched them, but the naive concept is probably the brainchild of the 17th-century print maker, who borrowed, mixed, and interpreted engraved material from a variety of existing printed sources without troubling to unify the various scales. A more sophisticated design concept, and therefore perhaps a later development, segregates the pictorial story within a central decorated cartouche, while confining the flowers, birds, animals and insects to the surrounding reserves.

The figurative characters, usually dressed in 17th-century costume, relate primarily to one of the following pictorial themes.

Allegedly worked in Wales, the panel may relate to the escape of Charles II after his defeat at the battle of Worcester. Three figures have been constructed, partly in relief and in-the-round, real hair being imaginatively used, particularly on the female. Innovative use has been made of metal strips, threads and purl, and the soldiers' armour features spangles. Needlelace has been used to make minute, glove-like hands, oak and other leaves with wired edges, and to cover wooden moulds for acorns. With a final flourish, the embroiderer has edged her work with bobbin lace. Courtesy of Brecknock Museum, Brecon, Wales. Size: 43cm x 33cm (17in x 13in)

Butterfly wings and flower petals fly 'in the air' on this pastoral panel, circa 1600, from the Burrell Collection, Glasgow Museums, Scotland. Even more significantly, the two central figures are padded and raised. Works of this type have caused some authors to claim that stumpwork originated in Elizabethan times. A similar panel in the Fitzwilliam Museum, Cambridge, England, has probably been designed, though not necessarily stitched, by the same hand.

- Biblical stories from the Old Testament and the Apocrypha
- Incidents from myths and legends, including the stories of Juno and her peacock, Orpheus charming the animals, Mercury and Pan, Pyramus and Thisbe, Alpheus and Arethusa, Orpheus and Apollo, Daphne and Narcissus, Paris and Pallas, Venus and Ceres, the judgement of Paris, and Diana and Paris
- Allegorical themes, including the four seasons, the four elements (earth, air, fire and water), the continents, the senses, and the virtues
- Single figures, and groups, portraying kings, queens, gentlemen and ladies, together with their retainers
- Commemorative events, sometimes pertaining to the monarch; these pieces often incorporate a date, but the date may refer not to the event but to the year in which the embroidery was worked.

Each 17th-century embroiderer used her particular skills to interpret these designs, sometimes with a beginner's simplicity, but more often with a virtuoso range of stitch and thread techniques which are fascinating to emulate today.

CHAPTER ONE

NEEDLEMADE FABRICS AND STITCHES

The raised embroidery of the 17th century bridges two stitch disciplines which have tended to operate independently for the past two or three centuries. The first, which might broadly be described as 'hand embroidery', relies on a ground fabric to support a range of decorative stitches. Needlelace, the other discipline, is capable of supporting itself in its finished state, though it requires a temporary fabric base during the working process.

Above all other styles of embroidery, stumpwork relies on many separately-worked fragments of needlelace for its rich texture, versatility and ingenuity. The technique has its origins in Elizabethan embroideries, but in 17th-century raised work these lace fragments not only clothe many of the embossed shapes, but rise above the surface of both the ground fabric and the embossed areas with unparalleled freedom and exuberance. This use of needlelace is the distinguishing feature of 17th-century work.

Other separately-worked needlemade 'slips', made with a range of embroidery stitches on linens, and satins, overworked with embroidery, played an important role in clothing elaborate embossed shapes, but the need to stitch these to the ground fabric, in order to avoid frayed edges,

made them less versatile than needlelace, which has an edge that will not fray.

The stitches chosen for this chapter mirror the work of the 17th century, but we have also included a few additional stitches, which might not have been used in 17th-century work, but which are compatible with it and will broaden the scope of a modern embroiderer. Although this selection is amply wide enough for anyone wishing to create a raised embroidery of this type, we would also expect an experienced embroiderer to experiment with others and, in addition, to incorporate a variety of machine embroidery techniques.

The seashore is a source of endless fascination to Jane Rowe, and it constantly features in her work, as in Too Rough for Shrimping. *Needlelace shapes, cordonnette, and couronnes graphically describe her seashore, with its breaking waves and sea spray. Size: 14cm (5½in) diameter*

The rich colour and strong figurative elements in a medieval manuscript inspired The Siege. *The authors used raised figures and 'slips' in the style of the 17th century, mixed with dyed and free-machined ground fabrics of silk. Size: 24cm (9½in) square*

13

Ground fabrics for embroidery

Raised embroidery of the 17th century was most frequently worked on cream or ivory satin, but linens, completely covered in laid and couched threads or with other stitchery, were also used.

The ideal ground fabric for a modern raised embroidery will be strong and free from stretch. It will be capable of remaining taut in a frame throughout the working process, like the skin of a drum, and have the tenacity to withstand the attachment of raised areas, repetitive stitching, and penetration by wire and metal threads. Medium-weight calico (cotton), unbleached and unwashed, is ideal in use and can serve as a standards guide when choosing other materials. Crewel embroidery needles or betweens will be adequate for general embroidery tasks. A leather needle and a fine beading needle, whichever is appropriate, will be used to attach fragments of thin kid and beads.

Threads

Small-scale definitive stumpwork is at its most exquisite when silk threads finer than 100/3in thickness are used for the needlelace and when the other threads, stitches and complementary techniques used in a piece are carefully balanced in weight to ensure harmony. A wide range of fine linen, cotton, silk, rayon and smooth metallic threads have been specifically created either for lacemaking, or for hand or machine embroidery. Irrespective of their intended purpose, they can usually be interchanged between these three disci-

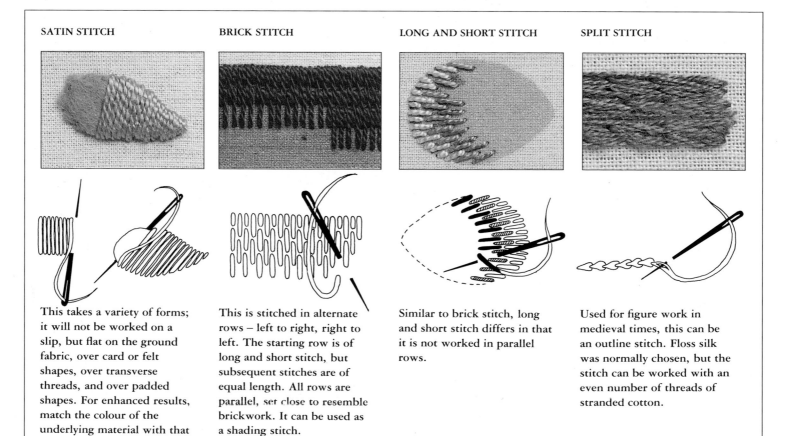

SATIN STITCH

This takes a variety of forms; it will not be worked on a slip, but flat on the ground fabric, over card or felt shapes, over transverse threads, and over padded shapes. For enhanced results, match the colour of the underlying material with that of the thread.

BRICK STITCH

This is stitched in alternate rows – left to right, right to left. The starting row is of long and short stitch, but subsequent stitches are of equal length. All rows are parallel, set close to resemble brickwork. It can be used as a shading stitch.

LONG AND SHORT STITCH

Similar to brick stitch, long and short stitch differs in that it is not worked in parallel rows.

SPLIT STITCH

Used for figure work in medieval times, this can be an outline stitch. Floss silk was normally chosen, but the stitch can be worked with an even number of threads of stranded cotton.

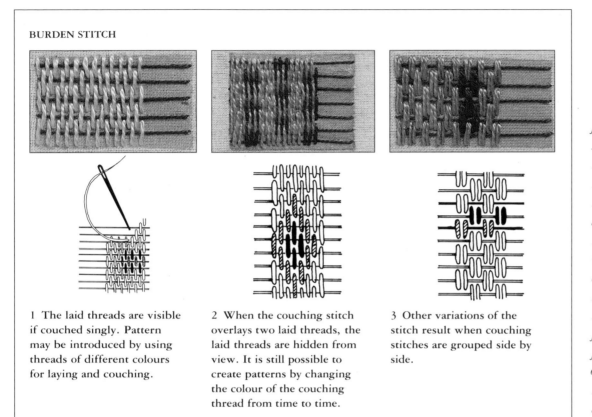

BURDEN STITCH

1 The laid threads are visible if couched singly. Pattern may be introduced by using threads of different colours for laying and couching.

2 When the couching stitch overlays two laid threads, the laid threads are hidden from view. It is still possible to create patterns by changing the colour of the couching thread from time to time.

3 Other variations of the stitch result when couching stitches are grouped side by side.

This embroidery, though faded, is rich in materials, stitches and techniques. It is thought to have come from Bingham Melcombe, in Dorset, England. Charles II and his queen, Catherine of Braganza, together with retainers, feature in the centre. Windsor Castle lies in the background, along with a lion and leopard, a parakeet, fish in a pond, and numerous flowers and insects. Courtesy of The Dorset Natural History and Archaeological Society, Dorset County Museum, Dorchester, Dorset

plines to suit the requirements of a contemporary stumpwork embroidery.

FLATWORK AND FILLING STITCHES

Five relatively difficult, though well-known, stitches provide a useful base. All can be used as 'flatwork' filling stitches but are also to be found overlaying embossed shapes on historic raised embroideries. In this latter form, most stitches must be worked on separate pieces of soft fabric – 'slips' – for subsequent attachment to the main embroidery.

The origins of burden stitch go back to the 14th and 15th centuries, but it was still very much in use in 17th-century English domestic embroidery. It imitates basketwork, with even-length darning or couching stitches, overlaying evenly-spaced laid cord-like threads.

LOOP STITCHES

For grassy mounds and landscape effects, 17th-century embroiderers kept largely to two stitch techniques. One is 'darned silk pile', which may be either cut or uncut. When cut, it resembles cut velvet stitch; uncut, it is somewhat like the upright gobelin stitch of canvas embroidery. (John L. Nevinson has suggested that this might be 'moss' or 'mosse' work, a term given to a lost form of groundwork of the Elizabethan and Stuart periods.)

The second technique is often referred to as 'unravelled silk', and has a coarse, curly texture that appears to be formed in loops and then possibly couched in a manner similar to that used for pendant couching. Theresa Macquoid, part-author of an early catalogue of the Lady Lever collection, tantalizingly tells us that this 'twisting of silk' is called 'springing', but provides no working guidance.

The only way to unravel these mysteries would be to dismantle a valuable embroidery, but in the absence of working methods for these two historical techniques, it is possible to achieve similar results by using pendant couching for uncut loop effects, and velvet stitch, either cut or uncut.

This tiny embroidery is remarkably rich in raised techniques. Unravelled silk is found at the bottom of the panel, while darned silk pile is seen both uncut and cut. Courtesy of Laing Art Gallery, Tyne and Wear Museum Services, Newcastle upon Tyne

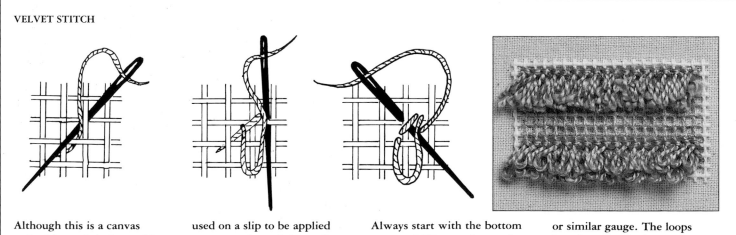

VELVET STITCH

Although this is a canvas embroidery stitch, it would need to be embroidered on a soft fabric if it were to be used on a slip to be applied over an embossed shape. One complete stitch is here shown in three working stages. Always start with the bottom row, and if loops of even size are required, make the stitches over a knitting needle or similar gauge. The loops have been cut in the upper part of the worked example.

One of two embroideries based on our photographs of sheep shearing in New Zealand, Sheep Shearing One *captures the atmosphere of the shearing shed, with its bolted timber beams, and the posture of a sheep shearer at work. The grid-like design is achieved with fabric paint on a calico ground, and machine stitching on a felt backing gives a lightly quilted effect. Numerous individually-worked slips covered with pendant couching, in slightly varied colours, are padded to represent sheep and fleece. Size: 18cm (7¹/8in) square*

PENDANT COUCHING

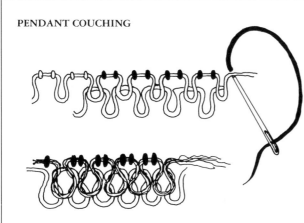

Worked freely on almost any type of fabric, the stitch consists simply of a thread, or group of threads, couched to the ground fabric in consecutive loops. Start with the bottom row, and ensure that the couching stitches are covered by the loops of an upper row.

KNOT STITCHES

Knot stitches are frequently to be found on 17th-century raised embroideries. They can be used singly or in large groups, either on the ground fabric or on separately-worked slips.

FRAGMENTS OF CANVAS EMBROIDERY

Along with other techniques, fragments of canvas embroidery are also to be found on 17th-century work. These were frequently embroidered as separate slips and then applied to the main piece. A less orthodox method is to attach a small piece of canvas, of the required size and shape, directly to the ground fabric, having first painted it in the desired colours. The canvas embroidery stitches pass through both the canvas and the ground fabric.

While this may not be acceptable to the purist canvas embroiderer, the method ensures a perfectly flat result, with no bulking of threads between the ground fabric and the canvas. Any small edge of canvas that is visible beyond the extent of the canvaswork stitchery must be hidden by other embroidery or some such means – the rather unsatisfactory 17th-century solution was to couch a cord around the edge. Many canvaswork stitches are suitable for raised embroidery, but we have restricted ourselves here to three which were popular in the 17th century.

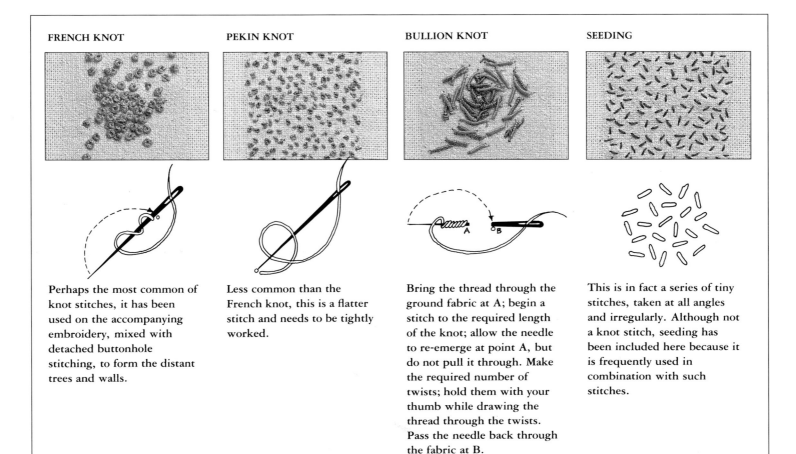

FRENCH KNOT

Perhaps the most common of knot stitches, it has been used on the accompanying embroidery, mixed with detached buttonhole stitching, to form the distant trees and walls.

PEKIN KNOT

Less common than the French knot, this is a flatter stitch and needs to be tightly worked.

BULLION KNOT

Bring the thread through the ground fabric at A; begin a stitch to the required length of the knot; allow the needle to re-emerge at point A, but do not pull it through. Make the required number of twists; hold them with your thumb while drawing the thread through the twists. Pass the needle back through the fabric at B.

SEEDING

This is in fact a series of tiny stitches, taken at all angles and irregularly. Although not a knot stitch, seeding has been included here because it is frequently used in combination with such stitches.

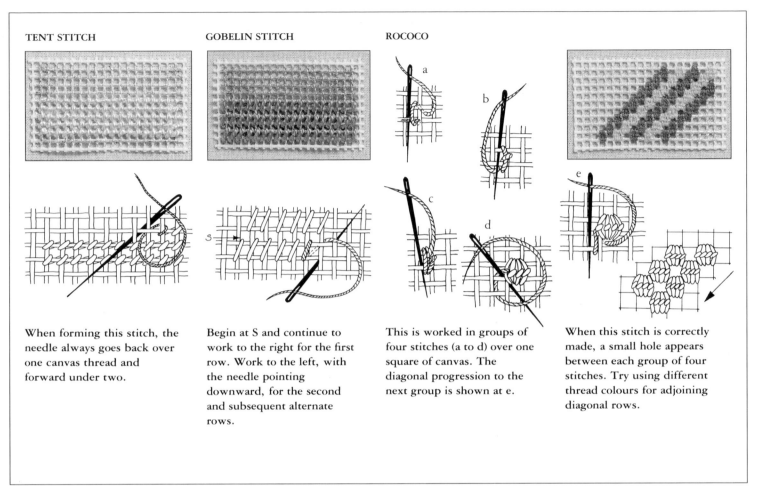

TENT STITCH

GOBELIN STITCH

ROCOCO

When forming this stitch, the needle always goes back over one canvas thread and forward under two.

Begin at S and continue to work to the right for the first row. Work to the left, with the needle pointing downward, for the second and subsequent alternate rows.

This is worked in groups of four stitches (a to d) over one square of canvas. The diagonal progression to the next group is shown at e.

When this stitch is correctly made, a small hole appears between each group of four stitches. Try using different thread colours for adjoining diagonal rows.

Barbara's first attempt at stumpwork embroidery, Tranquillity *has a spray-painted calico ground. The foreground is embroidered in a mixture of irregular uncut velvet stitch and bullion knots, while the sheep are in detached buttonhole stitch, worked on rows of running stitches. The tranquil lady is clothed with corded and single brussels stitches. Size: 20cm x 13cm (8in x 5in)*

CHAIN AND DETACHED STITCHES

Regular chain stitch is shown here, as are two variations. The second of these, raised chain band, is a detached stitch, in that the chain stitches do not pass through the ground fabric. The three other stitches are also detached, being worked on the upper surface of the ground fabric. The needlelace stitches which follow can be anchored to the fabric in this manner, if desired.

WHEEL FILLING

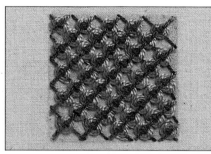

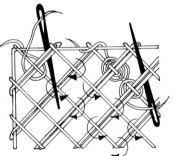

The wheels are woven into a detached grid of diagonal threads anchored only at their ends. Lay the double diagonal threads first, and then overlay these with single threads. Adjoining wheels always alternate direction. The wheels are worked in the direction of diagonal single threads, with the needle passing under double and over single threads (never into the ground fabric). On completion, weave the thread into the edge stitches.

CEYLON STITCH

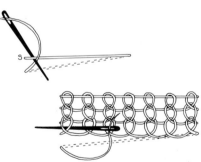

First form the bar: bring the thread up through the ground fabric at S; down through it again at any desired point, and then up again below point S. Loop stitches can now be made from left to right, as shown. These give the character of rib in knitting, and can be either tight or lacy. At the end of each row, the thread passes through and below the ground fabric, returning to the left end to start the next row.

HOLLIE POINT

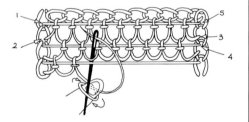

This is probably indigenous to England. First, form a chain or backstitched edge. Next, make a bar by bringing the thread up through the ground fabric at S, down again at 1 and then up at 2. The detached stitches are formed in loops over the thumb, as shown, and the working direction is from left to right. At the right edge, go down at 3 and up at 4, and then take the thread across to the left to the start of the next row.

CHAIN STITCH

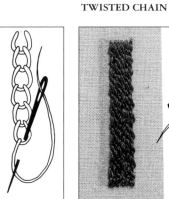

One of the most common surface embroidery stitches, this can be used as a filling stitch or as an edging.

TWISTED CHAIN

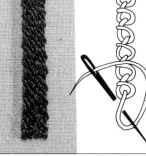

When formed in tight, directional rows, this can be used to suggest shape and contour in much the same way as split stitch on opus anglicanum.

RAISED CHAIN BAND

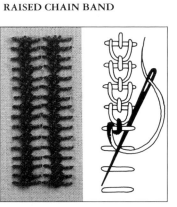

The bars of regular length and spacing may accommodate one or more rows of chain stitches. The bars pass through the ground fabric, while the chain stitches are worked onto the bars without going through the fabric.

Mary Anderson, equally at home with her sketch book or with needles and threads, sketched this all-too-familiar scene, entitled Embroidery '87, *at an exhibition in Bradford, England, and then translated it into an embroidered picture. Size: 28cm (11in) square*

21

NEEDLELACE FOR RAISED EMBROIDERY

Embroiderers are accustomed to applying stitches to and through a permanent ground fabric. Needlelace, however, requires no ground fabric, but relies on the way in which adjoining buttonhole stitches interlink, either with each other or with the edges of the lace, for support and continuity.

The edge of the lace is formed by a double, continuous thread, called a cordonnet. Each piece of lace is formed on a temporary foundation fabric with a shiny upper surface. We have found pvc/oilcloth fabrics the best for this purpose, but other materials, such as architect's linen, also work well.

The only stitches that penetrate the foundation fabric are the (also temporary) couching stitches that anchor the double cordonnet thread in the desired position. The lace can be made to almost any shape, including one with holes in the centre. When possible, use threads of the same colour for the cordonnet, couching thread and buttonholing.

A fine rust-proof wire, such as a fine beading wire

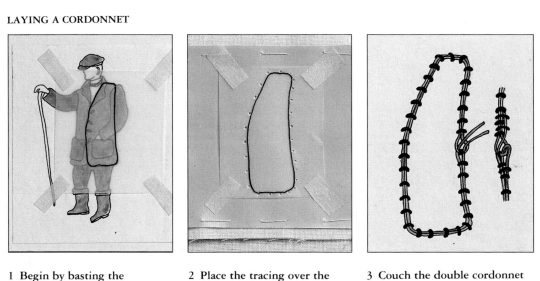

LAYING A CORDONNET

1 Begin by basting the temporary foundation fabric to two layers of cotton backing fabric – 15cm (6in) squares are a convenient size. Trace the required needlelace shapes from the design drawing; our example forms part of the farmer's duffle coat. Use either crewel needles or betweens for couching, and fine tapestry needles or ball point needles to make the needlelace.

2 Place the tracing over the foundation fabric, with a pad beneath, and, using a stiletto, pierce small holes through the pvc around the edges of the traced shape. If the finished lace is to fit over a padded area, make the holes just outside the traced outline. These pinholes mark the line followed by the cordonnet. Remove and discard the tracing paper.

3 Couch the double cordonnet thread over the line of pinholes. Knot the end of the couching thread; bring the needle up through the foundation fabric, and make the first couching stitch in the loop of the double cordonnet thread. Finish by threading and couching the ends of the cordonnet as shown. Couch thin beading wire with the double thread if the lace is to fly 'in the air'.

Roy's early life provided the inspiration for West Riding Pastures. *The working order for the embroidery was as follows: the calico ground fabric was brush-dyed with silk paints; with the ground fabric taut in a round frame, foreground meadow grasses and flowers were machined in free running stitch with a multi-coloured thread; the fabric was removed from the frame, backed with felt and quilted (free machining was used for the quilted wall and two distant sheep, while automatic straight stitch was used for the lines of distant hills). The embroidery was then returned to the frame and the stumpwork man and sheep were embroidered and attached. Size: 29cm x 27cm (11½in x 10½in)*

(similar to 5amp fuse wire), can be couched with the cordonnet if the finished piece of lace is to be only freely attached to the embroidery. This permits the lace to be shaped and manipulated, and to fly freely above the surface of the embroidery. Some writers speak of the lace being 'mounted on wire' or of wire being 'stitched to the edge of the lace' when referring to this technique. Hide the wire by button-

holing over the cordonnet when the shape has been filled but before it has been removed from the foundation fabric.

During the working process, the temporary foundation fabric is held in one hand, leaving the other free to make the needlelace stitches. If preferred, the foundation fabric can be attached to a drum, or needlelace pillow, leaving both hands free to stitch and control thread tension.

A NEEDLELACE STARTER STITCH

The essence of excellent needlelace is an even tension, and in *corded buttonhole stitch*, the long cord stitch that passes across the lace between each row of buttonhole stitches will help you to achieve this. Remember to pass the thread over and around the cordonnet at the beginning and end of each row, and also ensure that the buttonhole stitches along the finishing edge loop over the cordonnet. This total interlinking of stitches and cordonnet provides a kind of selvedge, adding strength to the needlelace. The starting and finishing ends of the working thread must be neatly worked into, and among, other threads of the cordonnet.

Helpful hints

- If the working thread is three or four times as long as the row, you will have sufficient thread to complete the row with enough thread left over to work it into the cordonnet to conceal the end.
- The type or colour of thread may be changed, but for simplicity this should occur at the beginning of a new row of stitches. When the rows are of varying colours, it may be necessary to select one of the colours to buttonhole the finished lace edge, giving it a neat and uniform appearance.
- Any buttonholing, picots or cordonnette on the edge of the lace, or other additional buttonhole trimmings, should be worked onto the lace before it is removed from the temporary foundation fabric.

    Regularly untwist the working thread to avoid knots and snarls.

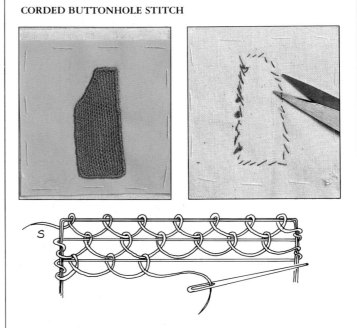

CORDED BUTTONHOLE STITCH

1 Having prepared the cordonnet, begin stitching at S. Fill the shape with corded buttonhole stitch, as shown in the diagram. The stitches can be worked across or down the shape; attention to this design consideration will enhance the pictorial quality of the finished work. When the shape is filled with lace, buttonhole over the cordonnet around the perimeter of the needlelace for an extra firm, neat finish. Only the couching stitches that anchor the cordonnet are allowed to pass through the foundation fabric.

2 When the lace is complete, it is removed from the foundation fabric: turn the fabric over and cut the couching stitches on the back. Still working from the back, remove the extraneous pieces of couching thread, using small pliers if necessary. Obstinate fragments of thread can often be dislodged if you cut the basting stitches that hold the pvc to the cotton fabrics and peel these layers apart.

MORE NEEDLELACE STITCHES

The four needlelace stitches given below might well prove sufficient for any raised embroidery, but they represent only a fraction of those that can be attempted. The *corded buttonhole variation* differs from corded buttonhole by the introduction of a second cord thread (using a second needle), which offers a means of introducing a second colour into the lace, with a resulting tweed-like effect. All these stitches are so straightforward that they require no explanation other than the stitch diagram, but you should note that the appearance can vary according to whether the stitches have been worked tightly or loosely, giving a lacy effect. By taking advantage of this, you will extend the range of application of each stitch.

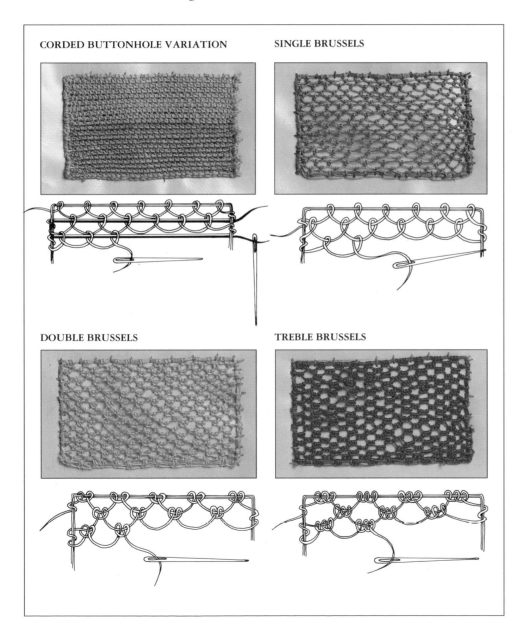

CORDED BUTTONHOLE VARIATION

SINGLE BRUSSELS

DOUBLE BRUSSELS

TREBLE BRUSSELS

This simple child study, Edwardian Children, *provides numerous stitch opportunities. Lacy treble brussels stitch on the girl's skirt contrasts with corded brussels; minute scraps of needlelace form a nosegay of flowers; a three-dimensional hat is composed of single brussels stitch and buttonhole stitching over card; and additional needlelace embellishments include pin picots and loop picots. Size: 21cm x 16cm (8in x 6in)*

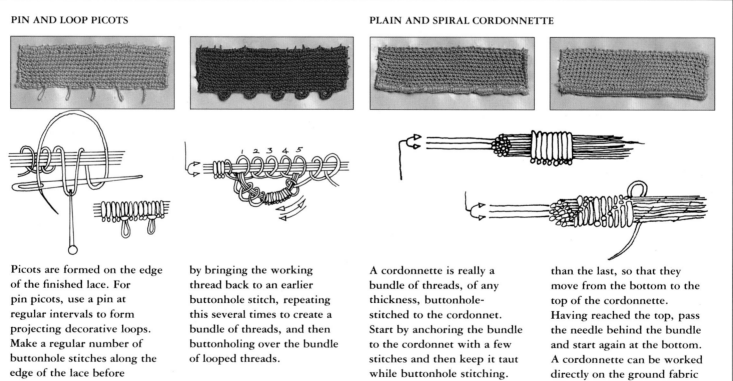

PIN AND LOOP PICOTS

PLAIN AND SPIRAL CORDONNETTE

Picots are formed on the edge of the finished lace. For pin picots, use a pin at regular intervals to form projecting decorative loops. Make a regular number of buttonhole stitches along the edge of the lace before working a picot stitch as illustrated. With the loop picot, the loops are formed by bringing the working thread back to an earlier buttonhole stitch, repeating this several times to create a bundle of threads, and then buttonholing over the bundle of looped threads.

A cordonnette is really a bundle of threads, of any thickness, buttonhole-stitched to the cordonnet. Start by anchoring the bundle to the cordonnet with a few stitches and then keep it taut while buttonhole stitching. The spiral effect is created when the knot on each successive stitch is set higher than the last, so that they move from the bottom to the top of the cordonnette. Having reached the top, pass the needle behind the bundle and start again at the bottom. A cordonnette can be worked directly on the ground fabric (start by couching down a bundle of threads).

Buttonhole trimmings

Each of the trimmings illustrated and described makes use of the simple buttonhole stitch. Although intended as appendages to lace, they can often be divorced from it and used by the raised-work embroiderer in unorthodox ways to decorate and embellish the embroidery.

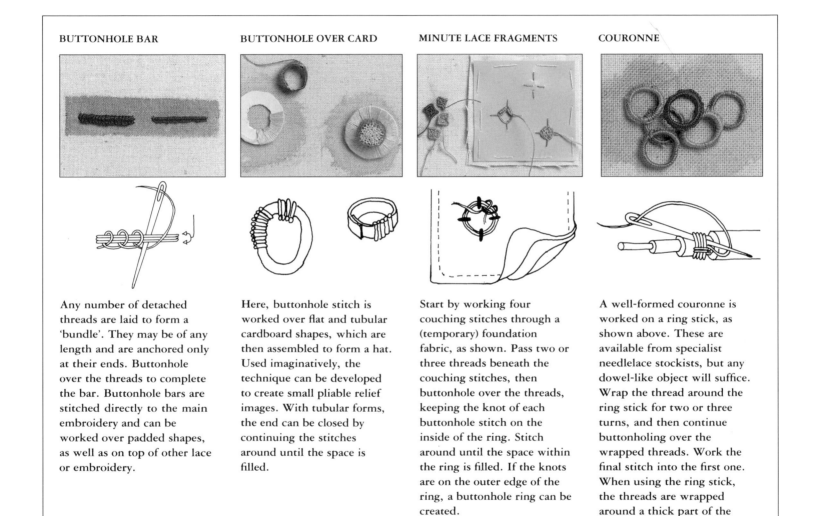

BUTTONHOLE BAR

Any number of detached threads are laid to form a 'bundle'. They may be of any length and are anchored only at their ends. Buttonhole over the threads to complete the bar. Buttonhole bars are stitched directly to the main embroidery and can be worked over padded shapes, as well as on top of other lace or embroidery.

BUTTONHOLE OVER CARD

Here, buttonhole stitch is worked over flat and tubular cardboard shapes, which are then assembled to form a hat. Used imaginatively, the technique can be developed to create small pliable relief images. With tubular forms, the end can be closed by continuing the stitches around until the space is filled.

MINUTE LACE FRAGMENTS

Start by working four couching stitches through a (temporary) foundation fabric, as shown. Pass two or three threads beneath the couching stitches, then buttonhole over the threads, keeping the knot of each buttonhole stitch on the inside of the ring. Stitch around until the space within the ring is filled. If the knots are on the outer edge of the ring, a buttonhole ring can be created.

COURONNE

A well-formed couronne is worked on a ring stick, as shown above. These are available from specialist needlelace stockists, but any dowel-like object will suffice. Wrap the thread around the ring stick for two or three turns, and then continue buttonholing over the wrapped threads. Work the final stitch into the first one. When using the ring stick, the threads are wrapped around a thick part of the stick, but are then slipped onto a thinner part to facilitate buttonholing.

CHAPTER TWO

PADDING, WRAPPING AND EMBELLISHING

An essential feature of raised embroidery is the formation, on the upper surface of the ground fabric, of embossed images with exactly the correct shape and level of relief. This is particularly true for any embroiderer attempting this style today; A. F. Kendrick, writing during the long dormant period during which this type of embroidery was out of favour, clearly doubted the success of 17th-century embroiderers. He refers to the 'grotesque ugliness' of the relief, calling it 'a mockery of sculpture' and claiming that this form of raised work was 'not the legitimate province of the needle'. Even the modern embroiderer or collector, who thoroughly appreciates this work, cannot entirely ignore the fact that it has a certain inelegance of form, compensated by the overall effect of the imagery, rich stitchery and ornamentation.

The soft padding materials used to create relief in the 17th century were diverse, but from early writers we can ascertain that they included unspun silk, wool, horsehair, cotton, tow and fabric scraps. Marcus Huish comments that the padding was held in position on the ground fabric with 'a lattice of crossing threads'. Also common, however, was the separately-prepared embossed shape, formed as an embroidered slip and complete with its own padding and pasted backing paper. The likelihood is that variety in both materials and methods was the norm, because embroiderers were innovating and experimenting in their efforts to achieve particular effects. In fact, relief was created not just with a range of soft materials, but also with harder ones, such as wax, wood, vellum and wire.

Today's embroiderers must use their judgement about such matters as when to use high or low relief, hard or soft edges, flat or bold and rounded surfaces, and the best means of achieving these. A range of materials and techniques are discussed, but there are many others that could be adopted or invented with equal effectiveness. Today's ideal soft filling will be a loose polyester (sometimes sold as terylene or dacron).

The ceremonial armour of the samurai, with its numerous separate protective lappets over body and arms, provides an excellent theme for raised embroidery.

The silk-bound wire hands of the Cellarer carry tiny gold leather keys and carved wooden bowl and jug. Leather lines the bowl, simulates pouring wine, and is also used for staves on the barrel and the decorative gold frame beneath pale blue spiral cordonnettes. Size: 17cm (6½in) square

SOFT, ROUNDED SHAPES

This is the kind of embossing that Marcus Huish described as 'padding held in position with a lattice-work of threads'. It can be used on either the upper or under side of the ground fabric, with dissimilar results.

Small running or backstitches are first worked on the ground fabric, around the outline of the shape to be padded. A latticework of threads, passing backward and forward over the shape, is then added, the thread being looped around the outline stitches. Soft filling is inserted between the fabric and the thread lattice as the work proceeds.

Felt shapes and soft padding are ideal for intricate shapes, such as the domes on Moghul Influence. *Size: 18cm x 6cm (7in x 2³⁄₈in)*

UPPER SURFACE PADDING

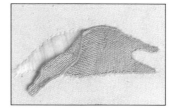

When the padding lies on the upper surface of the ground fabric, it can be made bold and rounded if the lattice stitching has been loosely worked. The embossed shape will be covered with a tightly-worked piece of needlelace, of matching (but slightly larger) shape. Set the initial running or backstitch outline just inside the design lines.

PADDING FROM UNDERNEATH

The main reason for padding from underneath is that the padded area can then be decorated with surface embroidery. Begin with the backstitched outline, and then fill in with embroidery stitching. Turn the work over, and pass the latticework of threads across the shape at the back, finishing by inserting the soft filling. The subtle effect of the low relief will only be fully appreciated when the work is mounted.

Padded slips

Overhanging or projecting features, such as the curtained tents on 17th-century embroideries, sit comfortably in relief and present no technical problems. Certain other relief features, such as the base of a wall, are only acceptable when matched by an equally heavily textured embroidery in the foreground.

Using felt and soft filling

Felt and soft filling are perhaps the simplest and most versatile of the materials used by today's embroiderers to form relief shapes with rounded upper surfaces. A single layer of felt beneath a piece of needlelace will be sufficient to create low relief, though the needlelace will sometimes have sufficient thickness in its own right and will require no assistance from other materials.

By far the easiest method when bold relief is needed, however, is to stitch a piece of felt to the ground fabric, and insert soft filling between the two.

PADDED FELT

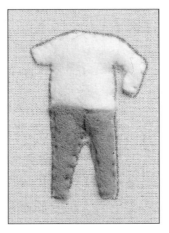 

Cut the felt shape no larger than the shape on the design drawing, and ease it inward when applying it to the ground fabric, stitching it inside the design line. This will create a pouch that will hold sufficient soft filling to give high relief. Add soft filling as stitching proceeds. To form an embossed base over which separate pieces of needlelace can be applied, it may be necessary to apply the felt in several pieces for ease of working.

APPLYING A SLIP

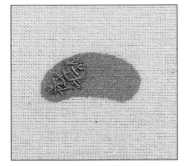  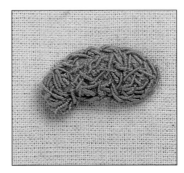

1 Slips are often padded. Embroider or encrust the surface of a (possibly) dyed slip with beads, metallic threads, purl or other decorative material. Use a soft fabric for padded slips.

2 Cut out the embroidered shape, leaving a 6mm (¼in) allowance all around. Make a line of gathering stitches around the edge and draw it up sufficiently to turn the edge under.

3 The slip can now be attached to the main embroidery. Insert soft filling beneath the slip as required.

FLAT, HARD-EDGED, LOW RELIEF

Stitch over the cardboard shape and through the ground fabric, keeping the threads close together and evenly spaced. Double-sided tape or dabs of glue will help to keep the cardboard in position.

Alternatively, apply double-sided tape to the underside of the cardboard shape, and bind it closely with thread. Stitch the bound shape to the ground fabric. This is quicker than the first method, and provides greater relief.

Here, the cardboard is sandwiched between a small scrap of fabric and the underside of the ground fabric, creating a very low relief effect. Anchor the cardboard to the fabric scrap with double-sided tape or glue. Pin or baste the two layers of fabric together and stitch around the edge of the cardboard with small, even backstitches.

The Village Butcher illustrates the use of several chain stitches, bullion knots, seeding and needlelace, as well as leather, wrapped card and fabric paints. One of the author's first raised embroideries, it was made with few preconceived notions as to how acceptable relief effects could be obtained. Size: 26cm x 22cm (10¼in x 8¾in)

FLAT, HARD-EDGED, LOW RELIEF

The three separate methods illustrated all use cardboard, from 1mm to 2mm (¹⁄₂₄in to ¹⁄₁₂in) in thickness, and various thicknesses of thread. For good visual results, use cardboard and thread of a similar colour for the first two methods, painting the card with watercolour if necessary.

Relief with metal

Each raised embroidery presents new problems that must be resolved. The tracery canopies shown right were created to overhang seated figures (see page 48), but variations of the technique shown will be found to have many uses in raised embroidery.

AN ELEVATED CANOPY

1 This working experiment shows a needlelace canopy on a temporary foundation. Note the short cordonnette with tassel. For *Majesty* (see page 48), metallic gold machine thread was used for the needlelace, with silk for the core of the cordonnette. Picots on the upper and lower edges of the canopy create the effect of masonry.

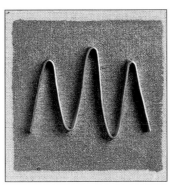

2 The seated figures are raised some 3mm (⅛in) from the ground fabric. To achieve the same lift for the needlelace canopies above the central niches, these were supported by a strip of soft metal, 3mm (⅛in) wide, which was bent to the correct profile, sprayed with gold paint, and stitched to the ground fabric.

Wire, flat soft metal, leather and threads

Plain stitching and binding over wire offer obvious possibilities to the raised embroiderer, and buttonholing over wire, with or without added picots, provides even greater potential for embellishment. Wire can also be used in combination with leather to form a semi-rigid and pliable structure, as can soft metal sheet, such as zinc or aluminium. Use rust-proof wire; select appropriate adhesives, and treat the raw, cut edges of leather with dye or fabric paint to enhance their aesthetic quality. The upper surface of the leather may also be decorated with inks or acrylic paints for added effects.

A strong pair of kitchen scissors will cut thin wire, but pliers with a cutting edge will be needed for thicker varieties. A tiny pair of the round-nosed pliers designed for

The embellishment of Samurai Four *started with the transfer-dyed satin fabric, which was overlaid with a bonded layer of silk organza, together with gold metallic paints and gold cords. The gold on the ground is mirrored by the gold leather on the warrior's armour, and the gold threads worked into the needlelace of the lappets. Size: 20cm (7⁷⁄₈in) square.*

ELABORATE STRUCTURES

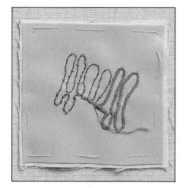 

SWORDS AND IMPLEMENTS

1 Elaborate wire structures should be bent to shape and couched to a temporary foundation fabric, then covered with buttonholing. Ensure continuity by stitching two or more wires together at strategic points. Remember that the only threads allowed to pass through the foundation fabric are the couching stitches. Select a wire of a thickness appropriate to the scale.

2 The main structure of this ancient Egyptian head-dress was created as described in step 1. Small spaces were filled with needlelace before the structure was removed from the temporary foundation fabric. The tiny fragments of gold leather were added to the embroidery as a final flourish.

A small piece of zinc sheet, cut and filed to the correct shape, forms the base for a sword or implement. A piece of gold or bronze leather is bonded to the upper surface of the zinc shape. When the adhesive is set and hard, a craft knife is used to cut away the surplus leather. Work with caution to avoid injury. Paint the raw edges of metal and leather.

An alternative method is to bond two thicknesses of leather together, sandwiching a piece of thin wire between the two. Cut the two pieces of leather as a matching pair; bond them with the wire; trim the edges with scissors or a craft knife when the adhesive has set, and finish by painting the raw edges to match.

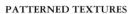

PATTERNED TEXTURES

Where one colour is used extensively, pattern plays an important role. Note how gold threads bound over metal strips and wires, twisted gold cord, gold purl, gold leather fragments and gold beads supplement the patterned textures of needlelace on *Majesty* (see page 48).

jewellers is invaluable, both for manipulating wire and for pushing and pulling the needles through ground fabric stiffened with stitching and padding.

Soft metal sheet, such as zinc or aluminium about 1mm (1/24in) thick is suitable as a base for forms in rigid relief. This metal sheet can only be cut with metal shears, and must be hammered flat after cutting and all cut edges filed smooth.

As with cardboard, apply double-sided tape to the underside of metal shapes to assist you when wrapping them with thread. Peel the protective paper away only gradually, as you bind.

SMALL LEATHER SHAPES

Thin, soft leather is available in a variety of colours, and with metallic surfaces, and the lighter colours will often accept silk dyes and other types of fabric paint.

To be in scale with other stumpwork images, leather will be used sparingly and in small pieces. It is of prime importance that pieces are of the correct size, and the following cutting method often proves satisfactory.

CUTTING SMALL SHAPES

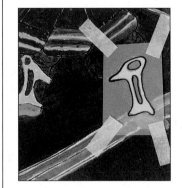
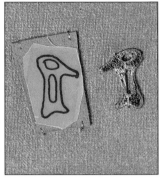

1 Start by tracing the required shape from the design drawing. If the leather is to cover an embossed shape, it may be necessary to increase the size a little. Cover the traced area with white glue and place the leather, wrong side down, over the adhesive.

2 Turn the leather-and-paper tracing side up, and cut around the outline, which will be clearly visible. Peel away the traced paper immediately after cutting. Paint or dye the raw edges of the leather for an enhanced result. Additional details can be added to the surface of the leather with indian ink and acrylic paints.

Fairy-tale Castle *is an unfinished work. The castle, which is padded with balsa wood, stands on a striped, flat, tent stitch slip, representing a ploughed field. The treescape is suggested by five embroidered padded slips in silver and mixed greens, worked in pendant couching, french knots, velvet stitch (cut) and bullion knots. Size: 10cm x 9cm (4in x 3½in)*

FURTHER TECHNIQUES WITH LEATHER

WOODEN MOULDS

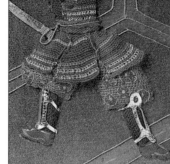

For shapes that are flat and hard, but pliable, leather can be bonded to thin cardboard. This is excellent for relief images, such as a top hat. Cut the shape with scissors or craft knife, making the cardboard slightly smaller than the leather, to help you to stitch the latter to the ground fabric. Crescent-shaped brims are cut to fit the shape of the raised head.

Soft, thin leather can be cut into intricate shapes with scissors, and then applied over needlelace or embroidery as an additional embellishment. Cut any inner holes first and finish by cutting the outer edge of the shape. Apply the leather to the embroidery either with decorative stitching or with the stitches concealed – under the lace, for example.

Another possibility is to insert soft filling beneath a leather shape to form a relief image. This is a useful technique for small details, such as hats or boots on figurative work.

These are of limited value, but can be useful when hard, straight, regular shapes are required – for the raised part of a building, for example. A few spots of glue will hold the mould in position on the ground fabric while it is covered with needlelace.

CHAPTER THREE

FIGURATIVE STUMPWORK

Much intricate and ingenious stitchery is used for foliage, flowers, birds, fountains and buildings on 17th-century raised embroidery, but the whole is brought to life by the small human figures and the stories they represent. Humour, pathos, anger and many other emotions are depicted in events from the Old Testament, the Apocrypha or Ovid's *Metamorphoses*, and although the stories are used over and over again, with only minor variations in design, our attention is held by the skill of each individual embroiderer.

While there is no point in copying the figures, costumes or stories from 17th-century embroidery, there is still a need to introduce figures into contemporary versions of stumpwork in order to create strong, absorbing effects. Figures in movement – athletes, for example, or rural craftsmen at work – provide opportunities to create embroideries that capture a sense of liveliness and excitement.

Keep the ground fabric tightly stretched in a frame while working, and complete any fabric dying, and stitchery on the ground, before starting the figurative work. It is possible to construct embossed images over some groundwork stitchery, but the task can be difficult. It is therefore preferable, for ease of working, and for economy of both time and materials, to stop the groundwork stitchery on the outline of the figure.

It is possible almost to complete some figures on a separate ground fabric and then transfer them to the main embroidery for finishing only. Figures which overlay other stitchery are best worked in this manner, but the technique also produces very bold embossing effects and has special values for this reason.

It is worth repeating at this stage that this embroidery is devised to create miniatures, and figures of appropriate scale will vary in height from some 6cm to 10cm (2½in to 4in). Smaller figures are difficult to work in the required amount of detail, while larger sizes can look ugly.

Larger pieces of needlelace can be crushed into smaller shapes to make a soft bonnet, as in this style of the early 1900s.

Watch the Birdie *is based on a 1920s photograph, taken at a golf tournament, which was recently reproduced in the* Daily Telegraph. *The action of the golfer, coupled with the postures of those in the small crowd, all gazing after the absent ball, make an excellent figurative composition. The figures are handworked, almost entirely in needlelace, and are further embellished with embroidery stitches, leather, and silk-bound wire. Size: 27cm x 30cm (10½in x 11½in)*

Embroidery frames

The chosen frame must hold the fabric taut and permit frequent adjustment. The authors prefer to use a round frame with a tightening screw and with the inner hoop wrapped with narrow bandaging or bias binding. Because the work is miniature in size, a frame with a diameter of 30cm (12in) is usually sufficiently large to hold the ground fabric. Alongside this we use a number of smaller frames, from 10cm (4in) to 20cm (8in) in diameter, to hold smaller pieces of fabric on which separate items can be embroidered.

BOUND-WIRE HANDS

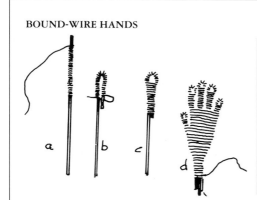

1 Each piece of wire represents a finger or thumb, and must be bound with silk thread for about 1cm (⅜in) at one end (a). Bend the bound end of wire, anchoring the loose end of thread in the bent wire (b). Overbind the bent end, as shown (c), and make four more. Leave a long thread on one finger and use this to bind the four fingers and thumb together (d) and to attach the hand to the ground fabric.

2 When binding, start by joining four fingers together, side by side; adding the thumb subsequently, and continuing to bind. Group the wires tightly together at the wrist before knotting off the thread. Cut away surplus wire, but leave a length of thread to overstitch the hand to the ground fabric, concealing it under the sleeve of a jacket or other garment.

Janny Bennitt chose a favourite photograph of her grandson and developed it into her treasured child study, David on a Trampoline. *Traditional techniques are used for the little boy, leather with bullion knots for the trampoline, and cretan stitches for the ground. Size: 13cm x 8cm (5in x 3¼in)*

With practice and patience hands, constructed as described, can be manipulated into a variety of forms on completion, as can be seen in The Quartet. *Size: 25cm x 20cm (10in x 8in)*

CONSTRUCTING HANDS

Although human figures on 17th-century raised embroidery are usually embossed, the hand sits most naturally when it is fully three-dimensional. Sometimes, a two-dimensional hand was embroidered on the ground fabric as an appendage to a raised figure, but this method is not a visual success.

At least three types of three-dimensional hand are found on historical stumpwork. The least common takes the form of a tiny needlelace glove, supported by an internal wire structure, and can be found on the Breknock Museum panel. The most widespread form is the wooden hand, and these were obviously obtainable as part of the 17th-century stump-work kit. The third historical method, and this is perhaps the most acceptable to today's embroiderers, is the bound-wire technique shown on the left. The thinnest wire and thread will create a very petite human hand, while slightly thicker threads and wire up to the thickness of a pin will produce a hand more suited to a working man. Avoid excessive binding, or the hand will be too large.

HEADS AND FACES

The head is usually the first part of the human figure to be embroidered on the ground fabric or applied to it. The soft-sculpture technique shown here is both versatile and lively. It was occasionally used in 17th-century embroideries, but the more common method was to stretch stitched or painted fabric over a small piece of wood or similar mould.

Materials

A well-washed, undyed cotton (calico, for English workers), medium to light in weight, together with soft polyester filling and natural-coloured thread are the basic materials used for heads and faces. The fabric on which the soft-sculptured head is constructed must be tightly stretched in a frame; round frames with adjustment screws are ideal.

Helpful hints

- Obtaining a head that is of a correct size for the design is often a question of trial and error.

- For best results, bring the needle through from the underside of the ground fabric slightly *outside* the line that defines the shape of the face and head; catch a tiny stitch into the edge of the slip as the needle passes back down through the ground fabric, at the same position.
- Insufficient soft filling will result in a flat, uninteresting face.
- The tiny stitches around the slip will be less obvious on a well-padded head.
- The eyes might appear to be too close to the chin during the early stages, but all will be well when the hair is added.
- The modelling of the finished head can often be improved if a needle is inserted through the fabric to lift and stir up the soft filling.
- The head can be applied either directly to the main embroidery or – where greater relief is needed – to a spare piece of ground fabric, for subsequent application to the main work.

Cindy Kurlansky used one of her nephew's drawings as her pattern for Farmyard. *He had intended to use the drawing to illustrate a book about his great-grandmother, but Cindy recognized its embroidery potential. Size: 19cm (7½in) in diameter.*

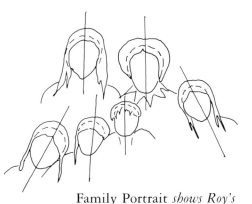

Family Portrait *shows Roy's mother and five elder sisters, and is based on a family photograph, dating from about 1916. It offered the chance to work through a range of ages, from baby to adult. All the heads were attached directly to the ground fabric. The correct size, position and inclination of each head, as shown in the sketch, are important keys to success. The largest head has a finished height of 1.8cm (¾in), and the smallest 1cm (⅜in). Size: 19cm x 14cm (7½in x 5½in)*

SOFT-SCULPTURED HEADS

1 Cut a small oval of cotton fabric; dimensions will vary but ovals are generally between 3cm (1¼in) and 2cm (⅞in) in height. With small stitches, run a gathering thread around the shape, about 3mm (⅛in) from the edge.

2 Draw up, turning the edge under, and knot. Decide at this stage whether the finished head will be the correct size.

3 The head shape is determined by the position of the needle coming up through the ground fabric and catching the slip with a tiny stitch. Stitch around the chin up to the mouth (halfway between chin and eyes). Push soft filling into the slip, particularly the chin. Anchor slip and filling with a tiny dot stitch at the mouth position.

4 Continue to stitch up both sides of the head to a point slightly above the eye position, midway between the chin and the top of the head. Add more soft filling, packing it down to join that already in situ. Make two more anchoring dot stitches, this time at the eye positions.

5 Continue stitching upward, packing the last soft filling in before completion. The stitches around the slip should be barely visible.

6 If the head is on a separate piece of fabric, it can now be cut away, with an allowance of 4mm (³⁄₁₆in). Gather this allowance, as shown; draw it up beneath the head, and stitch across with lacing stitches. Position the head on the main embroidery and stitch it in place – a few stitches will suffice.

Faces in profile

A good profile is more difficult to construct than a full face, even though they both start with a slip, as shown on the previous pages. It is therefore preferable to attach the profiled head to a separate piece of cotton fabric and then transfer it to the main embroidery on completion.

Riverbank, *an embroidery of two boys, seen in profile, was inspired by an illustration in* This England. *The heads were attached directly to the ground fabric, and the embroidery was all worked by hand, in a variety of stitches. The ground was lightly quilted. Size: 19cm x 14cm (7½in x 5½in)*

MAKING A PROFILE

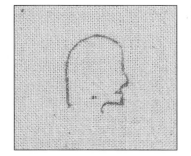 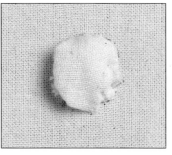 

1 Draw or paint a clear outline of the profiled head on a spare piece of fabric. To ensure that the painted line is covered, bring the needle up just outside the line of the profile; make a tiny stitch into the edge of the slip as the needle returns down through the same position in the ground fabric.

2 With the fabric taut in a round frame, begin stitching at the forehead. Following the profile, stitch down the face, finishing at the neck. Before making each stitch, manipulate the hem of the slip to make it adopt the shape of the profile. Push polyester soft filling into the shape, particularly the nose and chin.

3 Stitch around the crown of the head, and then down the back to the neck, adding filling as you go. Make a small dot stitch at the eye, which is close to the bridge of the nose. A chain stitch over the dot will form the eye, and a straight stitch makes the eyebrow. Attach the profile to the ground fabric as with a full-face head.

Embroidered features

The features and details are formed on the head in beige, brown, or grey/brown threads, placed over the dot stitches that already define the eyes and mouth. The two tiny dot stitches for nostrils are optional; sometimes they can be beneficial, but in general they can be omitted. Threads of a lighter colour tend to suggest youthfulness, and very dark threads are to be avoided.

Muted colours generally enhance the realism of the finished embroidery – choose a slate or a grey blue for blue eyes. Brighter colours can be useful for character effects, on a clown's face, for example.

The figures in The Stile *are set on a machine-embroidered ground, and the heads were constructed separately before being applied. Size: 23cm x 19cm (9in x 7½in)*

MAKING FEATURES

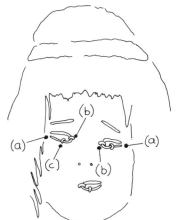

A chain stitch is worked at each eye, starting at the outer corner (a) and finishing near the nose (b). Draw the thread down quite tightly at the finish of each chain stitch to form a well-defined bridge for the nose. Move a thread of the chain stitch up or down to open the eye and lend character. Anchor with a dot stitch (c) where desired. The angle of the straight stitch for the eyebrow must be varied to give character.

The mouth can be formed with either a straight or chain stitch. The open, or singing, mouth is formed with a chain stitch anchored in the open position.

Two bullion knots, anchored in a crescent shape and one larger than the other, as shown, form excellent ears where these are necessary. The top of the ear is approximately opposite the eye.

HAIR STYLES

Threads, real hair, and metal purl can be seen on 17th-century raised embroideries, simulating the hair styles of the period. These days, thread and felt are usually sufficient.

The felt and the overlying threads must be of a similar colour. The function of the felt, which is roughly shaped to the hair style, is to form a raised pad, elevating the stitchery. Threads with sheen, such as rayon threads, are particularly suitable for the hair of women and children.

It is more important to create the desired impression than to copy slavishly from the design source. An intermixing of threads of two or more colours can provide highlights. The chosen threads will normally reflect those used for the embroidered facial features. Again, avoid very dark threads, as these are rarely effective.

Raised images tend to dominate an embroidery, but in Child in a Woodland Garden, *we have sought to give the influential role to the machine-embroidered frames, with their tree-like, leafy patterns. The figure of the little girl was worked in definitive stumpwork, completing the work on the ground fabric. Finally, the two leafy frames were loosely stitched to the ground fabric, one above the other. Size: 20cm (7³/4in) square*

In The Brothers, *one of the boys sits on a 'flat-work' chair. The relief and flat-work images combine successfully because the chair is shown in perspective. Although a three-dimensional chair would have been unworkable, it was possible to include a three-dimensional hat, so flat-work, relief and in-the-round images are all represented on this very small embroidery. Size: 14cm x 10cm (5¹/2in x 4in)*

BASIC STYLES

1 Cut small pieces of felt to the shape of the required hair style, and apply these to the padded head, working with the ground fabric tightly stretched in a frame.

2 Using the chosen thread, make directional straight stitches over the felt shapes until the felt is completely obscured.

3 The felt shapes can extend beyond the padded head to create flowing female hair styles, but directional straight stitches may be sufficient.

A good head shape, dense soft filling, and hidden stitches are essential features of a bald head. There is no longer any need to raise the hair with felt. The moustache is worked in raised satin stitch on the surface.

BEARDS

CREATING CHARACTER

KNOTS AND STRAIGHT STITCHES

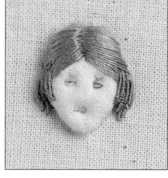

These are created in the same way as heads of hair. The shape is cut from felt; this is applied, and might need some filling below the chin line. In this example, straight stitches completely cover the felt. Bullion knots can be used as an alternative.

When making historical styles, study the appropriate contemporary sources. A solution of one part white glue to two parts water, plus a little ink or fabric dye, was applied to the head and face to give sheen and colour. About ten coats were applied with a small brush.

1 Straight stitches produce severe hair styles, whereas knots are rounded and soft, creating curls and ringlets. Here, straight stitches lie over felt, while french knots at the crown of the head are simply piled on top of each other.

2 Bullion knots, overlapping the ends of long straight stitches and placed at each side of a head, can provide a solution to hair styles requiring ringlets.

Ringlets of hair were made in groups and applied to the heads of the kings on Majesty. *To make ringlets, coat short lengths of silk thread with diluted white glue and wrap them in groups of about three around a thick needle or bodkin. Remove the needle before the glue has completely dried. The thread will now retain its curled ringlets.*

Majesty *is a raised embroidery inspired by the Gallery of Kings, at Lincoln cathedral. Size: 24cm x 22cm (9½in x 8½in)*

Long hair styles

Large numbers of separate threads can be knotted and pulled through from the underside of the ground fabric to produce elaborate hair styles. Some basic steps for a plaited style are illustrated, but other styles may evolve from drawing the threads through the ground fabric or head pad in varied positions. You might like to experiment with wool, unspun silk and other materials, such as real hair, to create special effects – make a sampler first.

A BACK PLAIT

1 A padded head, complete with felt hair shaping, has been prepared. An extra felt pad has been added near the top of the head to give more lift to the hair. A band of satin stitches follows the line of the hair, down the side of the face, ensuring that the felt will not be visible.

2 Pull three separate groups of threads through from the underside of the ground fabric: the top two groups are parallel, the upper being on the ground fabric and following the shape of the head, while the lower one comes through the padding; the third group also comes through the padding, and follows the edge of the face.

3 Draw the lower batch of top threads over the head and stitch them to the ground fabric at the nape of the neck. Trim away surplus thread.

4 Take the right-hand batch of threads horizontally to the back of the head and anchor it with a single stitch before bending the group down, where it is formed into a loop and stitched to the nape of the neck.

5 The final batch of threads is plaited and laid down the back of the head. Stitch the plait at the nape of the neck beneath the loop already formed, and trim away surplus thread. A needlelace bow and ribbons provide a final flourish.

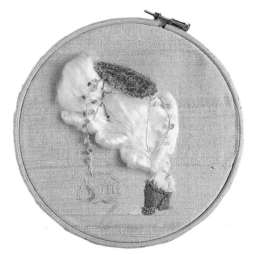

Anne Forbes-Cockel used unspun silk for her experimental Pompadour hairstyle, The 18th-century Roof Garden. *She has surmounted it with a parterre worked in french knots. Needlelace and bobbin lace garlands flow from the parterre, and a bobbin lace frill adorns the needlelace bodice. Her creation was inspired by an illustration in* London's Pride, *found in the London Museum. Size: 18cm x 13cm (7in x 5in)*

CLOTHING FOR FIGURES

An essential ingredient of success when clothing figures is close observation of the clothes or costume of the source material. Additional research, leading to a good all-round knowledge and appreciation of styles and materials, is also advantageous when you are trying to reproduce a costume in needlelace, in miniature form.

Most items of clothing will be created as a half of the real garment; occasionally it is better to reproduce virtually the entire garment, allowing parts to lie below the padded figure. Needlelace garments need not be tightly stretched over the padded figures; observe how clothing hangs loosely, or in folds, on the human form, and attempt to imitate this. To add to the richness of the finished effect, make and add tiny needlelace fragments for scarves, ties, collars, pockets, belts and handkerchiefs.

Four different techniques for making skirts are shown here, and some of these could be combined to offer an even greater range of effects.

The Vineyard is set on a lightly quilted and machine-embroidered cotton ground, dyed with silk paints. Size: 17cm (6½ in) square

MAKING SKIRTS

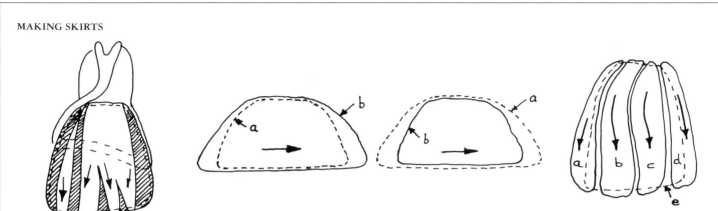

1 This method, used for *My Ancestors* (see detail), consists of a basic padded shape over which a single piece of needlelace is tightly stitched to the ground fabric. Bands of a darker colour are introduced to suggest the folds of a skirt, and this is emphasized by slight variations in stitch direction, indicated by arrows on the diagram.

2 Greater freedom results when the width of the needlelace skirt (b) is increased, particularly at the bottom. The sides of the skirt are stitched to the ground fabric, over the lightly padded shape (a), and the surplus width is gathered as it is applied, to fall into natural folds. Try to avoid stitching the bottom of the skirt to the ground fabric.

3 An even greater freedom results when an underskirt of needlelace is used for padding (a), as in this detail from *Edwardian Children*. The underskirt is stitched to the ground, inside the design outline (b), and held in place by a needlelace skirt, only slightly larger than the design outline. Neither should be attached to the ground at the hem.

4 A very different effect is achieved by building a skirt from several pieces (a–d) of needlelace, possibly wired at the edges. A lace underskirt (e), the size of the design outline, plus limited padding, will underlie the various pieces of lace. Again, the arrows suggest directional stitching. This method was used in *Majesty* and for the trilogy of monks.

Dressing a male figure

Before dressing a male figure, form the padded shape of the figure on the ground fabric (see page 31), just within the design lines. (The padded form is shown in hatching on the illustrations.) Choose felt of a similar colour to the overlying needlelace. Accurately position and attach the head, then add the cap. Work the needlelace pieces (a–k), testing for size by pinning them over the padded figure. Make a right hand (see page 40) and cut two leather boots. Finally, test the sizes, shapes and colours on the embroidered ground.

Mask the design lines on the ground fabric with the edges of the needlelace as the stitching proceeds. The arrows on the illustrations indicate the stitch direction which, in conjunction with the padding, will emphasize contour, relief and body movement.

BUILDING THE FIGURE

 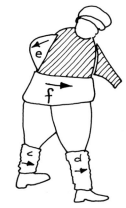  

1 Start by applying the trouser legs, a and b, in that order. The right (foreground) buttock may need a little more padding than the left. The left arm of the jacket (e) can also be attached at this stage.

2 Carefully apply the leather boots and two distorted needlelace puttees (c and d). The top and bottom edges of the puttees should overlap the trouser bottoms and tops of the boots without being attached. Apply the pullover (f), covering the trouser tops and stitching the sides only.

3 Apply piece g, covering the side of e, and form a good neck line. Apply piece h, but avoid tight stitching on the seam between g and h. The wire-edged bottom of the jacket will not be stitched to the ground fabric.

4 Insert the wrist of the wire hand under the felt at the bottom of the right arm; stitch the wrist firmly to the ground fabric. Ensure that the overall arm length and alignment is realistic. Now stitch the sleeve (j) in position, taking care to give the impression of an inset sleeve at the shoulder, and then add the pocket (k).

Freely intertwining silk-bound wires and soft kid, loosely applied to the ground fabric, set the scene for The Hedger. *Leaf-like kid shapes, small pieces of 'destroyed' skrim 'seeding', stitched to the ground fabric, and a stem-stitched hedge provide additional detail. An illustration in J.H.B. Peels'* Country Talk Continued *inspired the embroidery. Size: 25cm x 21cm (10in x 8¼in)*

Soft caps and hats

When you use the method for making a soft cap given below, you must start by either making the head, complete with hair, directly on the ground fabric, or applying a prepared head to the ground. A prepared needlelace crown can then be added. Extra padding will usually be needed in order to achieve the correct shape.

For a soft bonnet, slightly larger pieces (up to 30 per cent bigger than the finished size) can be crushed, resculptured, and loosely held in place with one or two concealed stitches. This technique was used for the child's bonnet on page 38.

A SOFT CAP

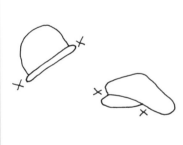

1 A cap peak or brim of a hat is formed with a wire edge. The wire ends of the prepared hat will penetrate the ground fabric at the points marked x. To do this, a small hole is made in the ground fabric with a stiletto; the wire is passed through the hole; bent flat beneath the ground fabric, and securely stitched beneath the head.

2 The wire edge for the peak or brim is first bound with silk thread, and then bent into a crescent shape and couched to a temporary foundation fabric. After buttonholing over the silk binding, two or three rows of needlelace are worked. Remove the work from the temporary foundation fabric.

3 Having inserted the wires through the ground fabric as already instructed, stitch the back edge of the peak or brim to the bottom edge of the crown. For the cap, the wire will also penetrate the padded head. Hat ribbons can be suggested either with several long satin stitches or with a narrow strip of needlelace, with added decorative embroidery stitches.

The brim for this hat is a straight piece of needlelace, slightly longer than the brim on the design drawing and about 5mm (³/₁₆in) wide. This is twisted, corkscrew-fashion, as it is lightly stitched over the bottom edge of the crown, which is already in situ. Minute scraps of needlelace, held in position with a french knot, can suggest a floral trim.

Wide-brimmed hats

The wide brim of a lady's hat provides an opportunity to make a wire-edged structure of the type frequently found flying from the face of a raised embroidery. Use wire the thickness of a pin, taping the ends to the foundation fabric to prevent the lace thread from snagging and to anchor the starting end of the thread. Remember that the only stitches allowed to penetrate the foundation fabric are the couching stitches that anchor the cordonnet or wire structure. All buttonhole (needlelace) stitches are detached, and lie above the surface of the foundation fabric.

The small crowd of eager buyers around a table of hats in a church hall in The Village Jumble Sale *provides an opportunity to illustrate the back of the lady in charge, but with her head turned to reveal a face in profile. Her head, like several of those in the crowd, was worked on a separate ground fabric before being transferred and applied to the main embroidery. Size: 22cm x 17cm (8³⁄₄in x 6³⁄₄in)*

MAKING A PROJECTING BRIM

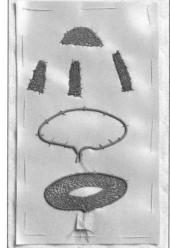

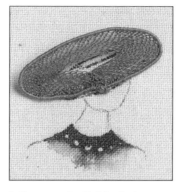

1 Start by tracing the hat crown (1), just outside the actual shape on the drawing or photograph. Trace the actual size of the decorative ribbons (2–4). Judge the shape and size of the brim (5), and draw it on tracing paper. Prick all these shapes on a temporary foundation fabric; lay cordonnets and make the needlelace for 1 to 4.

2 Cut a piece of wire some 6mm (¼in) longer than the circumference of the brim and bind it with silk thread. Bend the wire as shown; couch it over the pricked outline; buttonhole over the bound wire all around the brim (knots inward), and continue to work around until a small hole remains in the middle.

3 Remove the finished pieces of lace from the foundation fabric (see page 24). Accurately position the wired brim on the ground fabric and firmly stitch it in place along the lower edge.

4 Form a head slip and insert it through the hole in the middle of the needlelace brim. Accurately align the slip; stitch it to the ground; insert filling and define eyes and mouth (see page 43). Work alternately above and below the brim at this stage.

5 Stitch the needlelace crown over the padded head. Ensure a good stitched connection between the crown and the inner edge of the brim. Add features to the face and, below the brim only, stitches for the hair.

6 Finally, add ribbons and any other trims, then bend the wire edge of the brim to its final position.

CHAPTER FOUR

INSPIRATION, DESIGN AND DEVELOPMENT

A girl of the 17th century could rely on an intensive training in embroidery and needlelace stitches. She may have resorted to experiment rather than well-ordered practice for some raised embossing effects, but she probably relied almost entirely on other people for her designs and to transfer these to the ground fabric.

Many embroiderers today are accustomed to producing their own designs from original sketches, or from one of their own photographs. Source material for stumpwork designs, including figurative work, is also widely available in museums and art galleries, newspapers, magazines and brochures, and on posters, postcards, travel literature and advertisements. Whatever the source or subject this chapter suggests a range of basic techniques for preparing and developing the design, and for combining the embroidery with a number of other compatible skills.

As a first step, the design must be developed into a simple, yet bold, outline drawing, concentrating on the shapes that are relevant, and important, to the composition of a raised embroidery. It is wise to make about three copies of the design drawing. At least one of these will be on tracing paper, and this will be kept intact for reference, and to receive jottings and notes on threads, stitches, and tech-

niques as the work proceeds. Another copy will be used for pricking out shapes on the temporary foundation fabric and the final one might either be used for colour experiments or be cut into shapes and pinned to the embroidery to assess a likely effect. The design on the ground fabric is rapidly lost beneath padding materials as the work proceeds, and the tracing-paper design can be laid over the embroidery to position some slip or lace fragment yet to be applied.

Marilyn Chalke used an old photograph as the basis for The Tilemaker. *Size 18cm x 13cm (7in x 5in)*

A sepia photograph of Barbara's great-grandparents (seated), flanked by her maternal grandmother and great uncle as young children, inspired My Ancestors. *Correct facial shapes and postures are more important to this type of work than accurate likenesses. The female figure in the background is worked in twisted chain stitch directly on the ground fabric, with no padding except at the head. Various needlelace stitches clothe the other figures, which were made subsequently. Great-grandmother's shawl is in wheel filling stitch with a cut velvet stitch edge. Both children were made separately and then applied. Size: 21cm x 16cm (8¼in x 6in)*

TRANSFERRING DESIGNS TO FABRIC

A light box is a desk-like box with an internal light and an opaque glass top. It is invaluable for transferring a figurative design to fabric, but commercial models that are sufficiently large to be of use to the embroiderer are expensive. We have constructed our own shallow timber box, using a redundant piece of secondary glazing for the lid. Use a halogen bulb, to avoid the glass top overheating.

With the ground fabric taped to the glass top over the paper design, and the internal light on, the pattern will be clearly visible, and you will be able to copy it directly onto the ground fabric, either using a coloured outline or selectively dyeing areas.

If you do not want to make or buy a light box, try taping the design and fabric to a window. It may not be possible to dye the fabric when it is held vertically, but you can still mark the outlines.

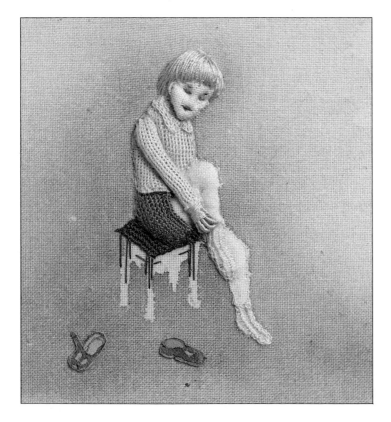

TRANSFERRING DESIGNS

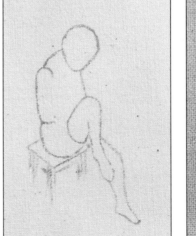 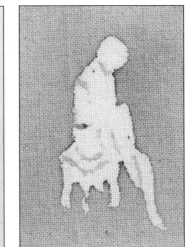

1 This design was outlined with gold metallic paint, applied with a watercolour brush. The outline must be accurately painted because it will determine the quality of the padded sculptural shape. Paint the size and shape of the head, not the outline of the hair. The positions of small features, such as the shoes, should be decided when the embroidery is nearing completion. An outline such as this can either follow an earlier dye process or be applied as a first operation.

2 In this alternative method the figure is voided, and the final result offers a decorative background, a design outline, and flesh-coloured legs for the young boy. Brush clean water into the hatched area of the unwashed and unbleached cotton ground fabric. Still using the brush, apply diluted fabric paint to the moistened area. The dressing in the fabric will act as a resist and prevent the paint from flowing onto dry areas. Practise this with various different paints and dyes.

Ian *was worked on unwashed, unbleached cotton. The boy's legs were outlined in backstitches and then padded on the underside of the ground fabric. He wears ceylon stitch socks. The stool is flat, and the shoes were cut from thin leather.*
Size: 13cm x 14cm (5in x 5½in)

Using transfer paints

Fabric transfer paints are designed for use with synthetic fabrics and are at their most brilliant when so used. While the results are more muted, they can, however, be successfully used to transfer patterns to other fabrics. Different brands of fabric paint have individual characteristics, and it is important to follow the manufacturer's instructions. Colours can usually be mixed and diluted.

The four basic steps to using fabric paints are as follows: draw the design on paper (do not use very thick paper); create a mirror image of the design, for example by holding it against a window and tracing over the outline on the reverse side; use a watercolour brush to apply the transfer paint to the mirror-image design, and leave this to dry thoroughly. Finally, place the painted design over the fabric and apply heat evenly, using a hot iron, to transfer the image.

Helpful hints

- The exact shapes of figurative images are difficult to achieve with transfer dyes – the hot iron tends to distort the fabric, producing a distorted image. It is usually preferable to transfer-dye the background design and then add the outlines of the figurative images in a metallic paint, using a light box.
- Colours are not predictable – test them on your chosen fabric before embarking on the design.
- The temperature of the iron, the duration of ironing, and the amount of paint applied to the paper will all contribute to the intensity of colour. Apply heat evenly over the whole area, and avoid keeping the iron stationary.
- The second print may often be subtler and therefore more usable.

USING TRANSFER PAINTS

The design work for *The Acanthus Invasion*, is here shown in three stages. The diluted transfer paints were applied to a soft porous paper, and the fabric is a polyester/cotton blend, of a natural colour. For accurate results, the outline of the figure has been added with gold metallic paint.

MAKING A SAMPLER

The stitches, techniques, threads, fabrics and other materials used to create a raised embroidery are all carefully selected to express, simulate and describe the subject. As a consequence, the choices open to the embroiderer are limited by the nature of the work.

If you want to make full use of the available options, you may well wish to begin by designing and making a sampler, filling it with as wide a variety as possible of figures, buildings, natural subjects (birds, trees and animals), imaginary creatures such as dragons, and numerous decorative stitches. A sampler of this type might be designed with a particular theme in mind – family, nature, the seasons, a period in history, or a particular event. Alternatively, a tiny raised embroidery, imitating a painted miniature, can provide a challenging opportunity to practise a surprising range of techniques in a very small area.

The suggestions offered in the next few pages provide possible starting points for your individual sampler.

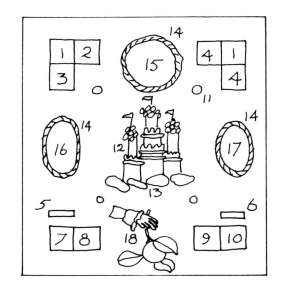

1 Corded buttonhole / mica window; 2 gold purl; 3 rococo; 4 burden; 5 silk bound card; 6 bound wire; 7 padded leather; 8 point de Venise; 9 treble brussels; 10 tent; 11 couronnes; 12 corded buttonhole, buttonhole bars, lace fragments, mica windows; 13 slips; 14 spiral cordonnette cartouche; 15 16, 17 soft sculptured heads, and 18 silk bound wire hand holding sprig of wire-edged needlelace leaves and a fruit in the round. Size: 25cm x 27cm (10in x 10½in)

Once Upon a Time imitates a building on a 17th-century stumpwork panel. Size: 16cm x 9cm (6¼in x 3½in)

Details on buildings

The finest buildings to be seen on 17th-century raised embroideries are not, surprisingly, drawn from English architecture. In all probability they are taken from earlier Flemish engravings. The success with which they are interpreted into raised embroideries stems from the tight groupings of numerous rounded and padded towers, sitting on embroidered and padded mounds. The towers are capped with fussy little roofs, covered with piles of needlelace tiles and peppered with windows permanently illuminated with mica. The recipe holds equally good for the modern embroiderer: avoid modern flat-fronted buildings, which offer no scope for raised work, and base your designs on buildings with turrets, towers and domes. A range of architectural samples and experiments is shown on the following pages, but the scope is endless.

SILK DYES

USING MICA

 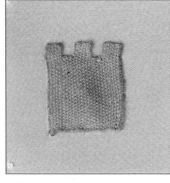 

1 Distinctive effects evolve when a colourless resist, obtainable from art suppliers, is used to outline shapes, controlling the spread of silk dyes. Use a light box (see page 58) when outlining with the resist, and stretch the fabric in a frame. Apply the dye with a brush, putting it in the middle of the area and allowing the dye to flow up to the resist line.

2 The same dyes can be applied to moistened pieces of needlelace, made from white or natural silk thread. Drop dye onto the lace, and allow different colours to flow and merge together. Dry naturally before heat-setting.

3 Alternatively, silk dyes can be used to space-dye threads. Wrap white or natural threads around your fingers to make small hanks. Moisten the threads, then use a brush to drop bands of dye onto the threads, allowing colours to merge. Dry naturally before heat-setting.

Mica, sometimes referred to as talc, is a naturally-occurring mineral with reflective properties and was much-used for windows and water in 17th-century work. Use old kitchen scissors to cut a fragment of mica slightly larger than the opening in the needlelace. Before applying the lace, stitch the mica over the felt or balsa mould with crossing threads which pass through both the padding and the ground fabric. Anchor the thread on the underside of the ground fabric. Avoid eye contact when using mica.

A raised composition merges with the adjoining ground when similar dyes are used for threads and fabric. Additional pattern is created when some threads are dyed before being used for lace, and others afterward, as in Windsor Castle. *Size: 20cm x 10cm (8in x 4in)*

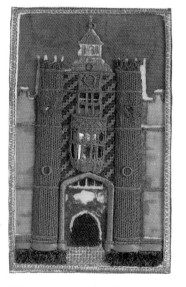

Flat canvaswork slips in rococo, tent and cut velvet stitch mix with needlelace, detached buttonhole bars, separately worked frames, buttonhole rings and leather to make Anne Boleyn's Gateway. *Balsa moulds give form to the towers. Size: 7cm x 12cm (2³/4in x 4³/4in)*

NEEDLELACE WINDOW DETAILS

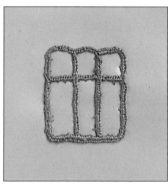

Emphasize window edges with buttonholing. Apply one or two detached threads to the lace across the window opening to make glazing bars. Buttonhole over these detached threads, which will overlay those anchoring the mica.

SEPARATELY-WORKED FRAMES

Couch a continuously interlocking pattern of several thicknesses of thread to a temporary foundation fabric, and buttonhole over this frame of threads. When removed from the foundation, the frame can be applied over needlelace or embroidery, once this is in situ on the ground fabric.

MASONRY DETAILS

Detached buttonhole bars can be worked over padded needlelace towers. Pass a few thicknesses of thread over the padded shapes, stitching through the ground at each end, and buttonhole over the detached threads. Alternatively, stretch narrow strips of leather over the tower, securing the ends only.

BIRDS

The parakeet, kingfisher and crested hoopoe commonly feature on 17th-century raised embroideries, along with the imaginary, dragon-like wyvern.

Similar birds and dragon-like monsters make equally good subjects for 20th-century work, offering scope for numerous overlapping fragments of needlelace, unlimited lace decorations and the use of exotic colours. The first step to designing a bird is to break the form into the separate, overlapping shapes that will be made in needlelace. Some will require a wired edge, allowing them to fly freely above the ground, being attached at one end only.

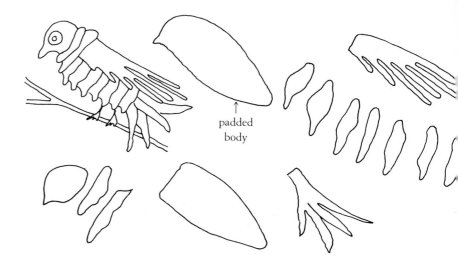

padded body

MAKING A BIRD

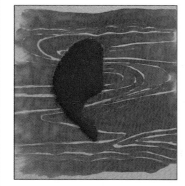

1 Use the felt and soft filling technique to form a padded head and body in high relief.

2 The pieces of needlelace shown here represent the underbody, head and neck, wings, tail and body feathers. Each piece was made from white threads and dyed after it had been removed from the foundation. Corded buttonhole was used in the main, but a few important sections were selected for decorative treatment.

3 Start by applying the needlelace for the underbody, following with the head and neck and then the tail feathers. Logically, work should proceed from the tail toward the head, but the order can be reversed if the wire-edged lace is lifted for pieces to be stitched below.

SHEEP

Sheep present interesting subjects for embroidery. The stitch detailing (probably pendant couching) and the padding will be greater if the animal occupies a foreground position, and in this case you might also choose to make a padded leather head. Distant sheep can be suggested with dye or very simple stitchery, while those in the middle distance may either be embroidered directly on the ground fabric or applied as slips. The thread thickness might be reduced, and although pendant couching might still be used, it could be combined with less heavily-textured stitches, such as french knots, or even with needlelace.

Here, raised sheep have been set against a background of felted sheep fleece. Size: 28cm x 20cm (11in x 8in)

A parrot-like bird features on the box from the Dorchester Museum. The drawing shows the various component parts used to create this effect, which include a padded body shape and many needlelace fragments, some with wired edges.

CONSTRUCTING SHEEP

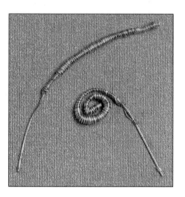

1 Keep the shape of the body simple when embroidering the slip – aim to produce a caricature. Narrow wedge-shaped pieces of leather form the legs, which usually look more realistic if they slope inward at the bottom.

2 The head is constructed on a piece of medium-weight cotton fabric stretched in an embroidery ring. Cut a head-shaped piece of soft leather; stitch this to the cotton, and pad boldly. Stitch the long, narrow eyes (note the position here), and add backstitches to sculpture the bony face and nose. Cut the head away from the cotton, leaving a turning, and apply to the ground fabric as for a human head (see page 43).

3 Firmly stitch the head over the padded body before attaching horns. To make a horn, unevenly bind wire with masking tape and then wrap this with thread, leaving some unwrapped wire at the root. Using a stiletto, puncture a hole through head, body and ground at the appropriate point; insert the wire end, bend it and stitch it firmly to the underside of the ground fabric.

TREES

Trees form an excellent subject for raised embroidery, and they also make good practice pieces. The pear tree stitch sampler shown on page 6, for example, included corded buttonhole, hollie point, tent stitch, pendant couching, single brussels, ceylon, french knots, velvet, chain, double brussels, rococo, seeding, split, chain band, treble brussels, burden, long and short, and twisted chain stitches.

A surprise gift, My Greenhouse *was based on Roy's secret sketches, photographs supplied by the owner's wife, and botanical illustrations. The relief figure stands in a flat-work greenhouse, filled with three-dimensional plants and tools. The ground fabric, a polyester/cotton blend, was transfer-dyed and machine-embroidered; the windows are of bonded organza; machine-embroidered leaves made on water-soluble fabric are loosely attached to the ground fabric, as are the tomatoes, which are stitched over spun cotton balls. All components were carefully placed to create the illusion of a three-dimensional greenhouse. Size: 29cm x 26cm (11½in x 10¼in)*

MAKING A TREE

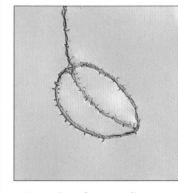 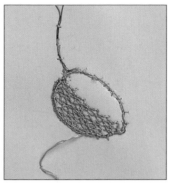 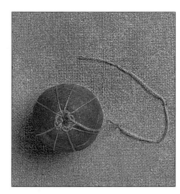

1 To make a free-standing leaf, first couch the cordonnet on a temporary foundation fabric and then add a thin beading wire. Take the wire all around the edge of the leaf and beyond, to form a stem.

2 Working from the central vein outward, fill half the leaf with the chosen needlelace stitch. Repeat, to fill the second half. Buttonhole around the edge of the leaf and down the stem.

3 For fruit, stitch a number of anchoring threads, segment-fashion, through a ball or mould made either of painted spun cotton or balsa wood. Pass two complete rounds of thread under the anchoring threads at one end where they enter the mould; buttonhole over this ring of threads, and continue to buttonhole around and around, linking with anchoring threads as necessary. You will need first to increase gradually and then to decrease the number of stitches.

4 Pass a double length of beading wire through the covered ball and anchor this with lace thread. At the other end, twist the wires together to form a stem, and then buttonhole over this. Add a fragment of needlelace to the bottom of the fruit.

5 Several thicker, silk-bound wires form the trunk and heavier branches. Fruit and leaf stems are either stitched beneath branches or inserted through concealed holes and secured to the underside of the ground fabric. Padded, embroidered slips hide the base of the trunk.

INCORPORATING MACHINE EMBROIDERY

Some textures and patterns of machine embroidery are in scale with, and can be used to complement, the hand-stitched techniques of raised work. The best results are likely to be achieved when the same, or similar, threads are used for both hand and machine techniques. Excessively heavy textures will probably conflict with the miniature scale of the designs, and for this reason should perhaps be avoided. Suitable machine techniques will include those listed on page 70, and in essence you will be drawing with the needle of your sewing machine.

True raised embroidery is here confined to the central medallion. The remainder of the ground fabric is machine stitched and relies almost entirely on pattern. The curved, waving lines of corn are lightly quilted; a decorative machine stitch forms the ears, and vermicelli stitch is easily recognized on the upper part of the panel. The Reaper *is a development of a roundel from a medieval manuscript. Size: 17cm (6½in) square*

LIGHT QUILTING

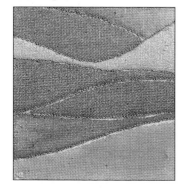

FREE RUNNING STITCH PATTERNS

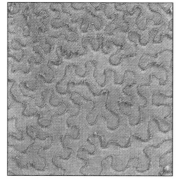
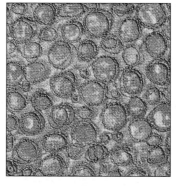

By stitching a layer of felt to the back, the ground fabric can be given a lightly quilted or sculptured effect. Baste the fabrics together with numerous rows of stitches in both directions. Machine from the middle, working outward. Use the feed dog and pressure foot for comparatively straight lines, but lower the feed dog and attach a darning foot for small, irregular shapes. These techniques were used on *The Reaper*.

1 Vermicelli stitch is a continuously reversing pattern of semi-circles. To create the necessary flowing rhythm, finish each complete area in one operation. Maintain a constant machine speed and constant, even movement of the embroidery, moving the frame with your hands. The scale can be changed, as shown.

2 Many additional filling patterns can be created, and you should experiment to find a pattern that suits the subject. The circular shapes seen above, for example, became a cobble-stone floor in *The Cellarer* (see page 29).

3 Free running stitch can also be used for natural forms, and here it is important to study the essential outlines and shapes. Move the embroidery at an irregular pace to achieve a variable texture, and remember to move it directionally to indicate the shapes of growing plants. Also bear in mind that you must create a sense of unity between the machine embroidery and the hand-stitching and relief shapes that will be added later.

- Light quilting effects achieved by backing the ground fabric with felt.
- Textured effects based on free running stitch; these can imitate natural forms, create patterns, or simply add texture.
- Free running stitch on water-soluble-fabric, used to create small lacy slips.
- Free running stitch on organza, or other flimsy fabrics, used to outline small slip-like shapes.
- Adding one or more fabric layers over the main ground fabric and machine stitching these together in design shapes and patterns, before cutting through some of the upper layers to reveal hidden texture, colour and pattern.

Free running or straight stitch

For this stitch, the fabric needs to be held taut in a circular frame during machining. Set the stitch length and width to 'O'; drop the feed dog, and either remove the pressure foot or use a darning foot. (Check the manual for your machine; the information is sometimes to be found under the heading 'Darning'.) Work at a reasonably high machine speed. To avoid excessively heavy textures, keep the embroidery frame moving the whole time and use fine threads. As the feed dog is no longer moving the fabric under the needle, you must move the frame around with your hands.

Machined slips and layers

The ground fabric of a raised embroidery can be enriched with an exciting range of techniques, including paints, dyes and fabric layers. Upper layers can be cut away to reveal lower layers of dyes, textures and fabrics, which will become integral parts of the overall picture. These effects are further enhanced if underside padding is introduced to create bas-relief. Further texture can be added to the upper surface of the ground fabric with machine stitching, or with applied slips that have been separately machined on a water-soluble fabric. (The hot-water-soluble variety is tougher, and more stitch-resistant, than a similar fabric, which will dissolve in cold water.) All these were used for *The Siege* (see page 13).

Machined layers of felt and fabric have been cut away to reveal hand-worked raised images on a dyed and bonded fabric.

PLANNING A WORKING SEQUENCE

Having prepared the draft design, study it with care; break it down into its various elements; attempt to plan a sequence for assembling the pieces on the ground fabric, and double check that you are absolutely satisfied that the design is capable of being translated into a raised embroidery.

The following steps describe the working sequence for the construction of *The Dancers*, which is based on a reproduction of a Moghul miniature. The conversion of this picture to a raised embroidery presented numerous challenging design problems, including the portrayal of the naked form, the intertwining of limbs and clothing, and the representation in needlelace of flimsy apparel.

Starting work
Inevitably, a high priority was given in the early stages to the creation of needlelace fragments, embroidered slips, and other features, all of which were ultimately to be attached to the main embroidery.

The fragmented parts of a raised embroidery are not easily assembled into a convincing naked figure. Inevitably, the joins between the various individual sections must be concealed under elements that are relevant to the composition. The alignment of the limbs and other parts becomes critical.

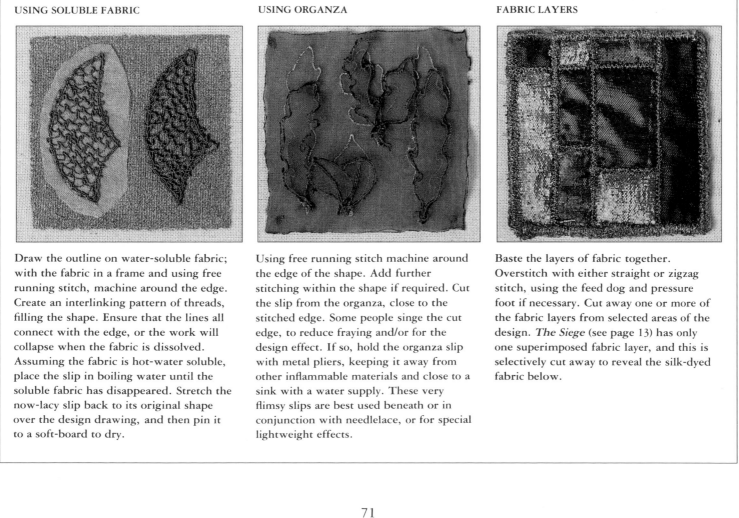

USING SOLUBLE FABRIC

Draw the outline on water-soluble fabric; with the fabric in a frame and using free running stitch, machine around the edge. Create an interlinking pattern of threads, filling the shape. Ensure that the lines all connect with the edge, or the work will collapse when the fabric is dissolved. Assuming the fabric is hot-water soluble, place the slip in boiling water until the soluble fabric has disappeared. Stretch the now-lacy slip back to its original shape over the design drawing, and then pin it to a soft-board to dry.

USING ORGANZA

Using free running stitch machine around the edge of the shape. Add further stitching within the shape if required. Cut the slip from the organza, close to the stitched edge. Some people singe the cut edge, to reduce fraying and/or for the design effect. If so, hold the organza slip with metal pliers, keeping it away from other inflammable materials and close to a sink with a water supply. These very flimsy slips are best used beneath or in conjunction with needlelace, or for special lightweight effects.

FABRIC LAYERS

Baste the layers of fabric together. Overstitch with either straight or zigzag stitch, using the feed dog and pressure foot if necessary. Cut away one or more of the fabric layers from selected areas of the design. *The Siege* (see page 13) has only one superimposed fabric layer, and this is selectively cut away to reveal the silk-dyed fabric below.

STORAGE

CONSTRUCTING BODIES AND FEET

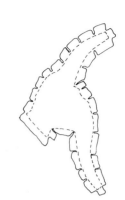

Ideally, most of the separate elements are prepared before the work of assembly commences. Being tiny, they are easily lost and must be kept secure. Small polystyrene trays make good interim containers. Alternatively, a piece of soft-board with the design drawing pinned to it can be used, both for storage and to give a visual check on progress.

1 Six shapes – the upper bodies and feet of the design drawing – are traced. Making the shapes slightly smaller than those of the drawing, they are cut from cardboard.

2 Lacing threads (see page 30) are wrapped around the cardboard to hold soft padding in place on the upper surface. The thickness of the padding can be varied in order to achieve a sculptured effect.

3 Cut a piece of undyed cotton fabric, slightly larger than the cardboard shape, and make snips around the edge as shown. Carefully stretch the fabric over the padded shape, gluing the allowance to the underside of the cardboard with white (children's) glue.

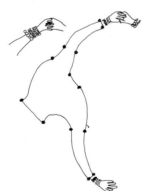

5 The joins betwen the wired hands and padded bodies, and between the heads and the bodies, are masked with numerous bracelets of strung beads. Those between ankles and legs are covered with needlelace. The soft-sculptured heads, upper bodies and feet are treated with a solution of diluted white glue with added dye (see page 47).

4 The upper body is attached to the ground fabric with a few stitches only. These are carefully positioned at points that will ultimately be concealed beneath later additions.

The finished embroidery of
The Dancers. *Size: 24cm x
18cm (9¹/₂in x 7in)*

Assembling the embroidery

A raised embroidery is built up in a series of layers. The lowest layer hugs the ground fabric and is the first to be applied. Succeeding layers must follow in the correct order of precedence. In reality, the process is a continuous one, with some flexibility in the working order, but for convenience, we describe it in three broad stages.

The first stage in the assembly of *The Dancers* was the attachment to the ground fabric of the skirts (1, 2, 3), part of the head scarves (4, 5, 6), and the separately-made heads. The angle of each head, and its placement in relation to the other, is of critical importance. The sashes (7, 8, 9, 10) could have been fixed at the point where they pass between the legs either at this stage or before the padded legs were formed (stage two).

At the finish of the second stage of the assembly, the two figures, although they were not worked as a whole, were finally linked together – by their clasped hands. Once again, the alignment of the various parts called for precision. The padding (felt with soft filling) for the lower body and legs was now applied directly to the ground fabric. Care was taken to ensure continuity between the parts. The needlelace trousers were now applied; sashes were attached to the waist, and the feet, needlelace braces, bangles, earring and necklaces were added.

In the third and final stage, the pieces of needlelace that project the furthest (11, 12, 13, 14, 15, 16) were added. The addition of the stylized goldwork paving below the dancers, together with a machined gold oval frame, completed the embroidery. Having stretched and laced it over soft board 1cm (3/8in) thick, the edge of the panel was embellished with gold metallic thread bound over a strip of metal 1cm (3/8in) wide.

The working sequence and assembly details will obviously differ for each composition, but the above should provide a useful general guide. Advanced embroiderers will also find it interesting and valuable to study as wide as possible a range of 17th-century raised embroideries. The lists on the following pages will hopefully suggest some possible sources of first-hand information.

To help Barbara with the design for Kathakali Indian Dancer, Yvonne Morton provided her with photographs of each item of clothing and jewellery, and of the male dancer in various stages of dressing. Tradition plays an important role, both in the way the costume is worn and in the dance, which takes place outdoors, at night, by the light of a lamp. The jewel-like adornments include minute scraps of needlelace, beads, mica, gold kid and metallic threads machined on a water-soluble fabric. A soft-sculptured head and other small features have a finish of acrylic paint. The embroidery is worked on a transfer-dyed satin ground fabric.

THE ASSEMBLY PROCESS

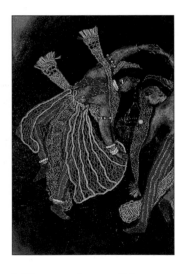

1 The first stage of the assembly process is not quite complete, but some items belonging to the second stage (upper body and necklace) have already been applied.

2 Here, the second stage of the assembly is not fully complete on the left-hand figure.

3 The second stage of the assembly process is almost complete for the right-hand figure, while the third stage has been completed on the left-hand figure.

APPENDICES

Biblical stories

The following is a list of biblical references used for the raised embroideries in some 28 museums surveyed by the authors.

Abraham	
and Eliezer	Genesis 15
and Hagar	Genesis 21
banishment of Hagar and Ishmael	Genesis 21
entertaining the angels	Genesis 18
offering Isaac	Genesis 22
Sarah and Isaac	Genesis 21
Adam and Eve	Genesis 3
expulsion from Eden	Genesis 3
Daniel and the lions' den	Daniel 6
David and Bathsheba	2 Samuel 11 & 12
Deborah and Barak,	
Jael and Sisera	Judges 4 & 5
Esther and Ahasuerus	Esther
Isaac and Rebekah	Genesis 24
Jacob	
and Laban	Genesis 28
Leah, Rachael and Laban	Genesis 29
his blessing	Genesis 32
his dream	Genesis 28
Jephthah	
and his daughter	Judges 11
and his rash vow	Judges 11
Joseph, sold by his brothers	Genesis 37
Moses	
finding of	Exodus 2
overwhelming of Pharoah's host	Exodus 14
Prodigal Son	Luke 15
Ruth, story of	Ruth
Saul, annointing of	1 Samuel 10
Solomon	
and the Queen of Sheba	2 Chronicles 9
judgement of	1 Kings 3

From the Apocrypha

Darius, his family before Alexander	Esdras
Judith and Holofernes	Judith
Susanna and the elders	Susanna
Tobias and the angels	Tobit

A Short Reading List

CABOT, NANCY GRAVES 'Pattern Sources of Scriptural Subjects in Tudor and Stuart Embroideries', *Bulletin of the Needle and Bobbin Club*, New York, vol. xxx, 1946

HAKENBROCH, Y. *English and Other Needlework in the Untermeyer Collection*, London, Thames and Hudson, 1960

HEAD, RACHEL E. 'The Decorative Embroideries of the 17th Century', *The Reliquery and Illustrated Archeologist*, 1902

HUGHES, THERLE *English Domestic Needlework 1660–1860*, London, Abbey Fine Arts, 1961

HUISH, MARCUS *Samplers and Tapestry Embroideries*, London, Longman Green & Co., 1900

JOURDAIN, M. *The History of English Secular Embroidery*, London, Kegan Paul, 1910

KENDRICK, A. F. *English Embroidery*, London, Batsford, 1904, *English Needlework*, London, A. & C. Black, 1933

MAQUOID, PERCY & THERESA *English Furniture, Tapestry and Needlework of the 16th to 18th Centuries*, London, Batsford, 1928

Men, Birds, Beasts and Flowers Exhibition Catalogue, Bath, Holburne Museum, 1987

NEVINSON, JOHN L. *V & A Catalogue of English Domestic Embroidery of the 16th and 17th Centuries*, London, H.M.S.O., 1938

'English Domestic Embroidery Patterns', Walpole Society, vol xxviii, 1939–40

'Peter Stent and John Overton', *Apollo*, November 1936

SELIGMAN & HUGHES *Domestic Needlework*, London, Country Life, 1926

SWAIN, MARGARET *Figures on Fabric*, London, A. & C. Black, 1980

'The Embroidered Box', *Embroidery*, Autumn 1987

List of raised embroidery collections surveyed by the authors

A prior appointment should be made to ensure either that the stumpwork is on display or that access to stored work will be available.

THE ASHMOLEAN MUS., Dept of Western Art, Oxford, OX1 2PH, GB

BANKFIELD MUS., Akroyd Park, Halifax, West Yorkshire, HX6 6HG, GB

BIRMINGHAM MUS. & ART GALLERY, Chamberlain Squ., Birmingham, B3 3DH, GB

THE BOWES MUS., Barnard Castle, Co. Durham, DL12 8NP, GB

BRECKNOCK MUS., Captains Walk, Brecon, Powys, LD3 7DW, GB

BRISTOL MUS. & ART GALLERY, Queens Rd, Bristol, BS8 1RL, GB

THE BURRELL COLLECTION, Pollok Country Park, Glasgow, G43 1AT, GB

THE CECIL HIGGINS ART GALLERY, Castle Close, Bedford, MK40 3NY, GB

THE ART INST. OF CHICAGO, Michigan Ave, Adams St, Illinois, 60603, USA

CONCORD MUS., PO Box 146, Concord, MA 01742, USA

COTEHELE HOUSE (NT), St Dominick, Saltash, Cornwall, GB

DORSET COUNTY MUS., High West St, Dorchester, Dorset, DT1 1XA, GB

FENTON HOUSE (NT), Windmill Hill, Hampstead, London, NW3 6RT, GB

THE FITZWILLIAM MUS., Cambridge, CB2 1RB, GB

GUILDFORD MUS., Castle Arch, Guildford, GU1 3SX, GB

HEREFORD & WORCESTER CTY MUS., Hartlebury Castle, Nr Kidderminster, GB

HOLBURNE MUS. & CRAFT STUDY CENTRE, Gt Pulteney St, Bath, BA1 4DB, GB

THE NATIONAL MUS. OF IRELAND, Kildare St, Dublin, Eire

LADY LEVER ART GALLERY, Port Sunlight, Bebington, Wirral, L62 5EQ, GB

LAING ART GALL., Tyne & Wear Museums, Higham Place, Newcastle-upon-Tyne, NE1 8AG, GB

THE MUS. OF LONDON, London Wall, London, EC2Y 5HN, GB

LOS ANGELES COUNTY MUS., 5905 Wilshire Boulevard, California, 90036, USA

THE METROPOLITAN MUS. OF ART, Fifth Ave at 82nd St, New York, 10028, USA

MUS. OF COSTUME & TEXTILES, 51 Castle St, Nottingham, GB

ROYAL ONTARIO MUS., 100 Queens Park, Toronto, Ontario, Canada, M5S 2C6

ROUGEMONT HOUSE, c/o Royal Albert Memorial Mus., Queen St, Exeter, GB

SALISBURY & SOUTH WILTSHIRE MUS., The Kings House, 65 The Close, Salisbury, Wiltshire, SP1 2EN, GB

NAT. MUS. OF SCOTLAND, Chambers St, Edinburgh, EH1 1JF, GB

SHELBURNE MUS., Shelburne, VT 05482, USA

CITY MUS. & ART GALL., Bethseda St, Hanley, Stoke-on-Trent, ST1 3DW, GB

ST EDMUNDSBURY MUSEUMS, The Clock Mus., Angel Corner, Bury St Edmunds, GB

SUDBURY HALL (NT), Sudbury, Derbyshire, DE6 5HT, GB

SUDELEY CASTLE, Winchcombe, Cheltenham, Gloucestershire, GB

VICTORIA & ALBERT MUS., South Kensington, London, SW7 2RL, GB

WADDESDON MANOR (NT), Aylesbury, Buckinghamshire, HP18 0JH, GB

WARWICKSHIRE MUS., St Johns House, St Johns, Warwick, CV34 4NK, GB

WELSH FOLK MUS., St Fagans, Cardiff, CF5 6XB, GB

WHITWORTH ART GALL., The University of Manchester, Oxford Rd, Manchester, MI5 6ER, GB

COLONIAL WILLIAMSBURG FOUNDATION, Williamsburg, VA 23185, USA

WISBECH & FENLAND MUS., Museum Squ., Wisbech, PE13 1ES, GB

YORK CASTLE MUS., Eye of York, York, YO1 1RY, GB

Chronological index of the authors' raised embroideries

Year	*Title*
1982	Tranquillity
	The Village Butcher
	Harvest Time (in the Embroiderers' Guild Collection)

Year	*Title*
1983	Sheep and Shepherd Box (at W. I. Denman College)
	The Garden Party
	Thumb Sticks (p)
	My Ancestors
	Family Portrait
	The End Of An Era (p)

1984	Brusher Mills (p)
	The Sand Castle

1985	Riverbank (p)
	The Brothers
	Once Upon A Time
	Windsor Castle
	Jumble Sale
	The Hedger (p)
	Samurai One (p)
	The Grave Digger (p)
	Sheep on Fleece

1986	Notely Abbey (p)
	Ian
	The Quartet
	Stumpwork Bird
	Three Dimensional Bird

1987	Majesty
	Shepherd and Sheep (p)
	Samurai Two
	Samurai Three (p)
*	The Cold Frame (p)
*	Commemorative New Zealand Box (p)

1988	Edwardian Children
	The Dancers (p)
	Samurai Four

Year		*Title*
	*	The Stile
		Heads Sampler (details)
		Hands Sampler (details)
		Padding and Wrapping Sampler (details)
		Pear Tree Stitch Sampler
		Anne Boleyn's Gateway
		Mogul Influence
	*	Sheep Shearer One
	*	Sheep Shearer Two
		Padding & Texture Techniques – Sampler
	*	The Acanthus Invasion (p)

1989		Heads and Hats Sampler (details)
	*	My Greenhouse (p)
		Kathakali Indian Dancer (p)
		Designs on Fabric Sampler
	*	Watch The Birdie
	*	The Siege
	*	The Gardener (p)

1990	*	West Riding (p)
	*	Pastures New (p)
	*	West Riding Pastures
		A Stumpwork Sampler
	*	The Ice Palace
	*	The Cistercian Reaper
	*	The Cistercian Cellarer
	*	The Cistercian Vineyard
	*	Hansel & Grettel

1991		Hat Sampler (details)
	*	Bleuet et Coquelicot
		Orange Tree and Sampler
		Exotic Bird
		Cordonnet Sampler (details)
		Plaited Hair Sampler (details)
	*	Child in Woodland Garden
		Fairy Tale Castle

* Embroideries worked jointly by Barbara and Roy Hirst. All other embroideries are worked by Barbara Hirst.
(p) Embroideries in private ownership.